A Journey of Sword and Spirit

Robert E. Wolfe, II

Ōkami Publications
Copyright © 2024 by Robert E. Wolfe, II
Illustrations by Rosanne Salomone Wolfe
Cover Photograph by Charles Hudson
Contributions by Peter Hobart and Rie Hashimoto Bailey

All rights reserved. No part of this book may be reproduced in any form without prior, written permission from the publisher or author, except in the case of brief quotations in articles or reviews.

The material in this book is intended for educational purposes only. No one should undertake the practice of self-defense or martial arts without qualified instruction and supervision, and an awareness of the criminal and civil limitations on the use of force in self-defense. The author, publisher, and distributors are not responsible in any manner for any injury or liability that may result from practicing—or attempting to practice—the techniques described herein. Any application of the information contained herein is at the reader's sole and exclusive risk. In consideration of the risk of injury to oneself and others, prior to engaging in any type of self-defense or martial arts program, it is advisable to consult both a licensed physician and a professional martial arts instructor.

This book was written, edited, and printed in the United States of America.

FIRST EDITION

ISBN: 979-8-218-42701-6

DEDICATION

For my wife, Rosanne, and our daughter, Erika,
without whose love and support this journey,
as well as Itten Dojo, would not have been possible.

CONTENTS

Foreword		i
1	History of Itten Dojo	1
2	The Gold Watch	27
3	Fight or Quit!	29
4	The Habit of Achievement	33
5	"Spiritual" Budo	37
6	Myths of Self-defense	43
7	Stupid, Stupid…	47
8	An Illuminating Fourth	51
9	Momentum	59
10	Why Form Matters	63
11	The Power of Words	67
12	The Frog in a Well	73
13	Why Iaido?	77
14	The Art of Letting Go	91
15	Why Nihon Jujutsu?	95
16	Reflections	101
Appendix—Law of the Fist		109

FOREWORD

Something remarkable happens when the right student meets the right teacher. The whole outcome of such a meeting is far more than the sum of its parts.

When I met my iaido teacher, Yamaguchi Katsuo Sensei, in 1988 in Las Vegas, I was struck by his physique and his charismatic energy. I resolved to train with him when I moved to Yokohama later that year and, after proving myself to Sato Shizuya Sensei (the late director of *Kokusai Budoin*, IMAF), I was able to do so. My first two-hour lesson with Yamaguchi Sensei was a pivotal moment. We connected in a way that I have never connected with a martial arts teacher—or with almost anybody else. He recognized my resolve; I was absolutely smitten with him. Yamaguchi Sensei represented everything I dreamed a martial arts instructor could be—extraordinarily talented, obsessed with iaido, kendo, and shodo, as kind and patient as the Buddha, and the best role model I've ever met for what a man, a husband, and a leader should be.

I have only half-jokingly said that if Yamaguchi Sensei had told me that I should throw myself in front of a train to get better at iaido, I would have done so without hesitation. I leave it to others to debate whether that level of devotion was healthy, but what it did for me was to remove any mental or emotional barriers to learning. I absorbed everything he taught, like an empty vessel. My time with Yamaguchi Sensei utterly changed the trajectory of my life. Despite his passing in 2006, the positive effects of knowing him continue to this day, not just for me, but also for my students and my family. After 56 years of martial arts, I live to share the blessings that Yamaguchi Sensei and other extraordinary martial arts instructors have given me.

Robert Wolfe reached out to me in 2018, and I traveled to his home, where I was treated to an extraordinary dinner prepared by his wife, Rosanne. We trained together that weekend, had a few conversations about the path forward for our collaboration, and gradually began to consider building iaido and Nihon Jujutsu programs for Itten Dojo.

Wolfe Sensei's dojo has had a long history. Not every path taken has led to a mountain top, but his senior cadre have every reason to be proud of their experience and abilities. It was clear early on, however, that he was looking for something more. He was not only looking for legitimate, heritage Japanese martial arts training, he was looking for an experienced mentor who would take a sincere interest both in his development and that of his dojo. In other words, he was the right student (if "student" is the right word for someone with such a vast body of experience).

At that stage of my martial arts life, I happened to be the right teacher. Something remarkable has happened in the six-year period we've been training and consulting together. Wolfe Sensei has seen the power and simplicity of the arts I've shared, we've become friends, and we've developed a delightful consulting relationship wherein I've been able to make suggestions about his training path and his development of Itten Dojo.

Let me not undersell the enormous part that Wolfe Sensei plays in this equation; it's critical to the point of this short narrative. He brings to the table an extraordinary work ethic, a martial intelligence borne of decades of experience, and a willingness to consider new ideas that you would have no reason to expect from someone who has accomplished as much in life as he has. He shares my vision for what's still possible, and that allows him to happily accept input and robustly apply it. Yamaguchi Sensei was at least 40 years older than I was, so it was no surprise to anybody paying attention that I accepted his teaching with such reverence. Wolfe Sensei is just a few years older than I, which might prevent a lesser man from accepting my guidance, but perhaps the fact that we are figuratively rowing the boat in the same direction together makes it a little easier for him to empty his cup.

One example of Wolfe Sensei's vast martial arts resume is this collection of stories from his writings in *Sword and Spirit*. He writes of meeting people, training, concepts, and history, and out of the writings emerges a keen sense of his place in the martial arts ethos of the last 50 or so years. There's a delightful balancing of tradition, reflection, and storytelling in this collection. You can see how intent he is to get to the heart of any matter, whether on the dojo floor or in a conversation with someone with expertise in something he wants to know about. And, tellingly, even within the 100+ pages of this book, you can see a little of his personal evolution and the evolution of Itten Dojo.

The outcome of our meeting is already greater than the sum of its parts. The hard work of getting better at iaido or at Nihon Jujutsu never ends, and there will be many obstacles ahead. As is said, however, "the obstacle is the way." The lessons to be taken from these delightful stories will help Wolfe Sensei, me, and hopefully you, as we navigate our paths forward. The right student does sometimes meet the right teacher. When that happens, it changes not only their own lives, but many lives, from their students to their families, and the generations that follow them.

Nicklaus Suino
Japanese Martial Arts Center
February 2024

1 HISTORY OF ITTEN DOJO

For as long as I can remember, I've wanted to train in martial arts. My father did some instructing of jujutsu while in the Marine Corps during World War Two, and while the few techniques he showed me when I was very young, along with his obvious respect for the Japanese as tough fighters, may have shaped my interest toward Japanese arts in particular, the interest in martial arts in general has always been there. My first real opportunity to train came when I was a freshman in college. Bucknell University required freshmen to take physical education, and in the spring semester, I took first boxing and then Shotokan karate. During summer vacation, I enrolled in the Isshinryu Karate Club (located initially in Mechanicsburg and then in Enola, Pennsylvania) and continued training.

The next school year, I organized and became president of a karate club on campus, training in Shotokan while at school and in Isshinryu while home on breaks. In addition, I became president of the university's European-style fencing club and a member of the judo club, so I was training in formal practices six days per week.

Following my graduation in 1978 with a degree in Japanese Studies, I continued with the Isshinryu club (which had moved to the Central Branch YMCA in Harrisburg), training under Ralph Lindquist, and tested for *shodan* (first-degree black-belt) in 1984. Eventually, several promotions later, I was chosen to succeed Lindquist Sensei as chief instructor of the club.

With Lindquist Sensei during a photo shoot for an article published in Black Belt Magazine by another local karate instructor, Tom Joerg.

During the time I was chief instructor, a number of the black-belts in the dojo became involved with professional kickboxing. Our fighters competed around the east coast, and my wife Rosanne (whom I met through the dojo) and I had the opportunity to serve as trainers and corner crew for an event in Maine that was televised by ESPN.

Isshinryu club black-belt/kickboxer Jim Kotzman, following one of his victories by TKO.

While kickboxing was a great deal of fun, it wasn't traditional *budo* (the martial Ways), and I found myself in the position of resisting the desires of most of the other black-belts to modify the training of the dojo as a whole to become consistent with ring-sport applications.

During this same time frame, we were heavily involved in publishing karate-related articles in a variety of magazines. Here, Rosanne Wolfe deals with a "mugger" in "Beating the Big Guy," from the April 1991 issue of Inside Karate.

A large measure of my resistance to shifting toward kickboxing was due to my exposure to more traditional arts, kenjutsu and aikijutsu. In the late 1970s and early 80s, I had subscribed to a little martial arts journal titled *The Bujin*, which was published by Fredrick Lovret, a kenjutsu/aikijutsu instructor in San Diego. I was delighted by the publication; more so when my first article, "Lessons from the *Gorin no Sho*" appeared in it in 1981. *The Bujin* ceased publication in 1982, and I heard no more of Lovret Sensei until the appearance of *The Way and the Power* in 1985. If I was happy with *The Bujin*, I was enthralled by *The Way and the Power*—the book purported to be a detailed exposition of classical Japanese strategy and I even based almost a year of karate classes on the principles described in the book.

When in 1990 I saw in *Black Belt Magazine* an announcement for a kenjutsu seminar with Lovret Sensei to be held in Washington, DC, I registered immediately.

The experience was startling. As my wife and I walked into the gymnasium where the seminar was being held, the very first thing we saw was a senior student rushing up to Lovret Sensei, dropping to a kneeling position, and presenting a hand towel Lovret Sensei had evidently requested. My reaction was, "Wow. These guys are *really* hard core." Which was exactly what I'd been looking for. I'd become accustomed to attending seminars and pretty much being able to do whatever was being presented regardless of the art; the seminar with Lovret Sensei was my first experience in a long time of feeling completely out of my depth, overwhelmed and challenged in a way that shook me deeply, to the extent that I almost didn't go back for the second day of the seminar. I did go back, and I was hooked.

I asked Lindquist Sensei for his permission to begin training in kenjutsu with the Maryland Budokan with William Knight Sensei, and although he said, "Okay," he clearly wasn't happy with the notion. Over the next two years, I made the mistake of trying to incorporate to the Isshinryu practice some of the elements and principles I was learning in kenjutsu. In other words, I was just as guilty of trying to alter the Isshinryu club as the black-belts who wanted to focus on kick-boxing.

The situation did not improve over time and so, in 1992 the Wolfes and the Starners made the difficult decision to leave the Isshinryu dojo. Within a week, the first practice of the Itten Dojo karate class was held on the second floor of the offices of Campbell, Rodoff, and Stewart Food Brokers on Trindle Road in Camp Hill, Pennsylvania (a building now long gone and replaced by a Chipolte Grill).

Alan Starner was a vice president in the company and had asked his boss, Mr. Bill Campbell, whether we might use part of the vacant upstairs while we looked for a permanent facility. Mr. Campbell had been a Lindquist karate student in the 1960s and was decidedly unhappy with us for leaving the Isshinryu dojo, but he agreed we could use the space for two weeks. Ultimately, we were there for seven years, long after the food brokerage was bought-out by other companies and gone from the building.

While we were all there, Mr. Campbell came to take great pride in the dojo. A tour of the dojo conducted by Mr. Campbell became a mandatory part of the first visit of any potential client to the offices of the food brokerage, and in one case landed the account when it turned out the client was an active karate practitioner ("Any company with its own dojo is exactly who I want to be doing business with..."). Mr. Campbell's active support made it possible for us to build the enrollment and resources necessary to move into a permanent facility. We regard Mr. Campbell as kind of the patron saint of our dojo, and still keep a photograph of him in our third (and current) facility.

First practice of the Itten Dojo karate class, September 29, 1992. From left: the author, Debra Starner, Rosanne Wolfe, and Alan Starner.

Our dojo evolved from a "mat" outlined in masking tape, to 24 tatami mats, then to 48 tatami, and finally to 60 tatami. This was an "open mat" practice, with both aikijutsu and kenjutsu students training.

Another person we always remember is Ted Vollrath, the founder of Martial Arts for the Handicapable and my karate instructor following our departure from the Lindquist dojo. Vollrath Sensei was known throughout the world as the first person to achieve black-belt rank in karate from a wheelchair, having lost his legs to wounds received as a Marine during the Korean War. Ironically, Vollrath Sensei's first karate instructor was Lindquist Sensei. In the years prior to his death, Vollrath Sensei provided the karate students in our dojo with an inspiring example and training opportunities in a variety of arts taught by his truly vast number of friends. Even after our karate class was disbanded, Vollrath Sensei continued to support the dojo with exceptionally perceptive advice and unfailing encouragement. Right up to the day he died, despite being in extreme discomfort, Vollrath Sensei concerned himself entirely with what he could do for others—his last conversation with me ended with, "If there's anything I can do for you, pick up the phone."

Vollrath Sensei visiting our first dojo for a promotion ceremony, with a very serious Erika Wolfe looking on—to her, he was "Grandpa Ted."

During the time we were at the Campbell building, the dojo evolved in significant ways. Kenjutsu and later aikijutsu were added to the class schedule and karate was eventually dropped entirely. For a while, we shared our space with the Gypsy Dragon School of Tai Chi, while that group built sufficient enrollment to enable leasing their own space.

Barbara Paul leading taiji training. She actually trained in Shotokan karate with the same instructor I trained with while at college.

The Lovret organization at that time was a growing enterprise, and to manage the far-flung dojo, Lovret Sensei decided to purchase a recreational vehicle and make two trips around the country each year, teaching week-long seminars at every dojo in the group.

Lovret Sensei instructing, during a seminar visit to our original dojo.

During this same period, we began publishing Tenshin-ryu/Yamate-ryu articles in a variety of magazines, primarily for the purpose of propagating the organization and, at the request of Lovret Sensei, undertook publication of *Koryu Budo*, the official, quarterly journal and monthly newsletter of the ryu. These actions had the effect of putting the organization before the public, but with consequences that were considerably different than those anticipated.

Within a month of my signing the lease for our second dojo, to be constructed in the lower level of an office building in Enola, Pennsylvania in the fall of 1999, the first big, anti-Lovret campaign exploded on the Internet. I was aghast—the new dojo wasn't even finished being built, and I could just see it all being swept away. We'd known there was some controversy attached to Lovret Sensei prior to the Internet attention; accusations of his never having actually trained in kenjutsu or aikijutsu, let alone trained in Japan, and having just made-up both arts. But I was stunned by the intensity of the anti-Lovret sentiment.

In a face-to-face, personal conversation, Lovret Sensei told me that no disclosures of his training history and experiences would be made—he made it very clear to me that he had severed ties with the Japanese with whom he had trained, did not wish to acknowledge them in any way, and that he did not regard his personal history as being anyone's business. In his words, "Look, I have not told you the entire story. I will *never* tell you the entire story. But everything I have told you is true, exactly as I have told you." By that criterion, I accept as true his statements that he had trained in Japan and that the largest Yamate-ryu practice he ever attended in Japan had a total of five people on the mat.

When, in a subsequent phone call, I made the point that I had just committed myself to a commercial lease totaling more than $100,000 and thousands of dollars in build-out expenses for the new dojo, and all of that (as well as financial ruin for me, personally) was now at risk, Lovret Sensei's response was, "Individual dojo are expendable." That statement was thoroughly chilling, and although we tried to soldier on in the absence of any other immediately obvious course of action, we started to consider whether we might have other options.

What we took to be a positive consequence of the Internet controversy was our meeting Richard Tolson, an instructor living in Dayton, Ohio. Mr. Tolson was a frequent poster on the martial arts discussion boards, and since his background was similar in some respects to that of Lovret Sensei (which is to say he had supposedly trained in a small, family system of classically-derived martial arts), he offered some words of encouragement. Tolson's Arashi-ryu was said to have been the creation of Tanaka Kajiro, an associate of Tolson's father, and with whom Tolson trained from the time he was a pre-teenager until he was in college.

We invited Tolson Sensei to teach a kenjutsu seminar. The event went very well, and Tolson Sensei's demonstrations of other portions of the Arashi-ryu curriculum were impressive, so we formed a study group to train in the Arashi-ryu. We remember the subsequent weekend spent on an introduction to the aikijujutsu portion of the curriculum as one of the most physically demanding seminars we've ever experienced. Despite the intensity and potential danger of the exceptionally dynamic techniques, there were no injuries whatsoever.

Tolson Sensei grinning at the sight of Randy Manning bouncing Ed Dix off the mat, during an Arashi-ryu aikijujutsu seminar.

Around the same time, a few of the members of the dojo began traveling to New York City to train in Daito-ryu aikijujutsu, and they eventually decided they wanted to pursue practice of Daito-ryu full time.

Our introduction to the Daito-ryu came through Rod Uhler. Rod grew up in Mechanicsburg and had trained in karate with Vollrath Sensei. After service as an Army Ranger, Rod moved to Japan to train in traditional budo and ultimately became one of Okabayashi Sensei's most senior and highly-ranked students in both aikijujutsu and kenjutsu

(Okabayashi Sensei's most-senior student was Hashimoto Mitsuko—she eventually became Mrs. Uhler). But they didn't want to quit our dojo, so I suggested that we request permission from Okabayashi Shogen Sensei to start a Hakuho Kai study group. Permission was granted, and we hosted our first visit from Okabayashi Sensei in the fall of 2000.

Okabayashi Sensei during his first seminar visit to Itten Dojo.

With the birth of their daughter, the Uhlers decided to move to the United States. At one point we expected Rod and Mitsuko to settle in our area, and we seriously considered having them become instructors at our dojo and converting everything to Daito-ryu and Ono-ha Itto-ryu (Sokaku-den).

Rod and Mitsuko Uhler teaching kenjutsu at the second Itten Dojo.

Instead, the Uhlers moved to Michigan. When it became clear to the Daito-ryu study group that the dojo overall would not transition to Hakuho Kai, the study group left the dojo to set up shop on their own. Subsequently, Okabayashi Sensei became sufficiently fed up with the constant infighting within the Daito-ryu "community" to drop the Daito-ryu affiliation altogether and he founded Hakuho-ryu Aikibudo.

The watershed event in the process of our first leaving the Lovret organization occurred early in 2001. I had posted on our website an article presenting the "history" of the Tenshin-ryu. When attacks on the article began, I asked the author for his documentation and was very disappointed to discover that most of the "sources" amounted to no more than stories told by certain seniors in the Tenshin-ryu. I pulled the article from the site, but not before it was read and commented on by Meik Skoss, a noted practitioner of aikido and various *koryu* (old-style arts). I was offended by one of Mr. Skoss's remarks, a snide comment that was particularly disparaging of the members of our dojo as individuals, but I had no idea how to respond.

All I could think of to do was to invite the Skosses to teach a seminar at our dojo, so they could meet the people who had been the subject of Meik's remark. I contacted Ellis Amdur, a close friend of Meik, with whom I had on occasion corresponded and whom I had found would always treat me squarely. I told Ellis what I had in mind and asked for his advice. Ellis had some questions for me, and after discussion agreed to raise the idea with Meik. After a bit more maneuvering, I was put in direct touch with Meik and we began to make plans for an introduction to *jodo* (focusing on use of the four-foot staff), figuring that topic would be least likely to conflict with either our kenjutsu or aikijutsu fundamentals.

It took several months to get everything together, during which time Meik and I started to get to know each other and increasingly enjoy our interaction through e-mail and over the phone. By the time the seminar arrived in July 2001, anticipation on both sides was keen, and as it turned out the event far exceeded our expectations. We all had a blast—Meik really liked the dojo and our members, and training with Meik was for us a bit of a shock after the rigid hierarchy and formality attached to training in the Tenshin-ryu and Yamate-ryu.

We knew we wanted to see more of each other and undertake training in jodo, but we weren't quite sure how to manage that. Meik told us he'd discussed the situation with Phil Relnick Sensei, and that it was decided we could train as individuals in *Seitei-gata Jodo*, a modern derivative of koryu Shinto Muso-ryu Jo, but there could be no formal recognition of our dojo by the koryu so long as the dojo was part of the Lovret or Tolson organizations.

Everyone figured that, by getting together once in a while, it would take us about two years to get through the modern portion of the curriculum, at which point we would have to make a decision: We could either stay as we were and content ourselves with just the Seitei-gata Jodo, or we could cut our existing ties in favor of formal training in Shinto Muso-ryu Jo. During this same time period, Rosanne and I met Diane Skoss when we spent a weekend at the Skosses' home in August 2001, and Diane came to our dojo in September for her first weekend seminar here.

Meik and Diane Skoss, with members of the Itten Dojo and Shutokukan Dojo Shinto Muso-ryu Jo classes.

During the seminar with Diane, and especially when Alan and I took Diane to dinner that Saturday evening, we had a chance to talk at length about the future course of our dojo. We reached the point of knowing what we wanted to do, if not exactly knowing how we were going to do it. While Meik was adamant that we should take full advantage of the time allowed to make a decision as important as leaving the Lovret organization, Diane made it plain she thought we should just jump ship and get on with it.

Concurrent with these events, a particularly outspoken, arch-critic of Lovret Sensei posted on several prominent budo web forums a satirical piece titled, "Levitating Kenjutsu Master." This article featured a photo of Randy Manning and me taken from our website and purported to be an interview with me in which I related how, after years of striving to suspend disbelief in relation to Tenshin-ryu, I found I could physically levitate myself at will.

The "levitation" photo. A sequence from a long kata during which the "defender" blocks two, rapid cuts while jumping. This was not easy.

I decided at that point I simply wanted to be able to focus on training, in whatever art, and no longer have to deal with the controversy. We had scheduled a seminar visit from Lovret Sensei for October 2001, but before the end of September we simultaneously paid his honorarium, cancelled the visit, and resigned from the organization. We also resigned from the Arashi-ryu.

I felt like "Neo" in *The Matrix*, running for the edge of the roof and taking the leap...

All members of the dojo were briefed on our choices and allowed the opportunity to comment or voice concerns before the resignation. In the end, we lost two people over the decision to resign from the Lovret organization. For everyone, there was an initial period of uncertainty and confusion, but as things settled down and people began to see the opportunities before us, the spirit of the dojo started to rebound. Still, the transition was far from easy, entailing as it did the thorough reinvention of the dojo.

Initially, we continued to train in the kenjutsu and aikijutsu classes pretty much as we had, while making adjustments to the curriculum and dropping any references of connection to a ryu. Meik came back to the dojo in February 2002 for a weekend seminar devoted to his *Toho*, a generic form of swordsmanship derived from the Zen Nippon Kendo Renmei (ZNKR) Kendo Kata and intended primarily as an introduction to swordsmanship for students of arts without an emphasis on weapons. Over the course of the next year, we combined Meik's toho with the ZNKR iaido taught to us by Pam Parker of the Ken-Zen Institute in Manhattan to build a fairly comprehensive introduction to swordsmanship.

Pam Parker instructing John Mark in seitei iaido.

The prohibition on entering a koryu had ended with our departure from the Lovret/Tolson organizations, our regular trips to the Skosses' Shutokukan Dojo in New Jersey resulted in our working through the probationary Seitei-gata Jodo more quickly than we had anticipated and, all of a sudden, a number of us found ourselves officially training in an authentic koryu. Over time, our jodo group became an increasingly active part of Relnick Sensei's organization, with a number of us traveling each year to the Pan-Am Gasshuku in Port Townsend, Washington, and our dojo hosting the eastern regional gasshuku (the "Least-West" Seminar) in October 2003. This event was called "the best organized gasshuku I've ever attended" by one of the most senior members of the Relnick organization—which was kind of an ironic assessment, considering we ran the weekend in accordance with everything we'd learned helping Knight Sensei host the Tenshin-ryu annual *Taikai* ("Great Gathering") at the Maryland Budokan.

We still had the problem of what to do with the aikijutsu class. After his having played so great a role in the reformation of our dojo, it seemed only proper to invite Ellis Amdur to visit and meet face-to-face. Ellis consented to teach an aikido seminar in January 2003, one of his patented blends of proper ukemi, practical atemi, and the principles of training with integrity. It was another milestone, and by the end of the weekend we knew we had a plan. Ellis agreed to become the technical advisor to our aikido class, assisting us in developing a curriculum suited to our dojo. Ellis continued to visit our dojo several times a year for the next five years.

Another major event we facilitated in January 2006 was a two-day seminar (kenjutsu and aikido) Ellis presented at the late Josh Freeman's Tomon Dojo near Gaithersburg, Maryland. (Josh had converted an old barn on his family's farm to a truly spectacular training facility, with a large mat area, dressing rooms, and guest quarters for visiting instructors.)

Ellis Amdur instructing at the Tomon Dojo, 2006. A friend from SMR Jo days, Joe Montague, serving as uke.

This seminar was very well attended, and participants included several individuals who had been highly and very publicly critical of the Lovret organization in the past. After having the chance to actually train with members of the Tenshin-ryu and Yamate-ryu, some of these fellows amended at least a few of their opinions—and even said so publicly in the same Internet forums they'd used previously for criticisms.

Overall, our experience training in Shinto Muso-ryu Jo was incredible. Not only was Relnick Sensei an astonishingly talented technician and instructor, he was an absolute gentleman and a sterling example of all that a sensei should be. Our affiliation with him also provided opportunities to not only train with but get to know personally fellow students of the ryu that were prominent in their own right, including Dave Lowry, one of my all-time favorite martial arts authors.

In the introduction to his excellent book, *In the Dojo*, Mr. Lowry mentions visiting a college bookstore in Ohio and purchasing a field guide to Amish buggies. This was actually during a Shinto Muso-ryu Jo seminar held at Kenyon College—to buy the book Mr. Lowry needed to bum $20 off me because he'd left his wallet in the dorm. The money was promptly repaid but I still think I should have gotten a mention, too!

That seminar weekend was also the second time we had the chance to train with Nishioka Tsuneo Sensei, one of the eight men awarded Shinto Muso-ryu Jo menkyo by Shimizu Takaji Sensei. Nishioka Sensei was in his late-80s when we trained with him, and he was utterly inspiring. At our first seminar opportunity to train with him, a few of us were individually given 30-minutes of private instruction by Nishioka Sensei (with Mrs. Nobuko Relnick translating). This experience stands as one of the highlights of my martial arts career.

We were exceptionally fortunate to receive some private instruction at the Kenyon College seminar, as well. The focus of training there was the Shinto-ryu kenjutsu that is a component of Shinto Muso-ryu Jo. The original kenjutsu within the ryu—sword vs. sword rather than sword vs. staff—was lost at some point over the past 400 years. If I remember correctly, the kata in Shinto-ryu kenjutsu were "reconstructed" in the 1800s, based on the use of the sword in the Jodo kata. During a break, rather than socializing as pretty much everyone else was, Alan Starner and I were burning reps of the kumitachi we'd been taught. Nishioka Sensei noticed what we were doing and came over to give us corrections and a much deeper level of details than had been provided in the regular seminar sessions with the entire group.

Relnick Sensei and Nishioka Sensei demonstrating during the seminar at Kenyon College. In the background, John Mark observes.

Unfortunately, difficulties ultimately arose that made it necessary for Itten Dojo to resign from the Shinto Muso-ryu organization, in December 2006. While there was an option available for us to maintain our affiliation with Relnick Sensei directly and continue training with him in Shinto Muso-ryu, the option was not especially viable given the requirement to commute 3,000 miles each way to his dojo in Washington state.

Consequently, we focused on the development of our aikido program while exploring different ideas for a complimentary study of traditional weapons.

We had tried a koryu-derived weapons practice with Ellis, but that did not prove viable, either. Next, my very good friend Mike Fontenot (Foothills Budokai, Denver, Colorado) opened to us the opportunity to train in a line of Muso Jikiden Eishin-ryu (MJER) iaido. Although the logistical challenges associated with that effort proved insurmountable as well, we learned a tremendous amount. The style to which Mr. Fontenot belonged practices a unique blend of traditional iaido and kata-based *tameshigiri* (test-cutting). This combination is an exceptional recipe for learning proper cutting, along with careful control of *maai* (distancing, or interval).

For a couple years, we tried to carry on through with a generic sword practice based on the Skoss toho and fundamental MJER kata. But that path wasn't very satisfying either—I wanted to train in a koryu school of swordsmanship, not make do with something I engineered myself.

And then I received an email from Rod Uhler, letting me know he and Mitsuko would soon be moving to the United States, and that as soon as they were settled in Michigan, they would like to fulfill a promise to teach a special seminar at our dojo. Rod proposed one day of Daito-ryu and a second day of kenjutsu, focusing on the *Gogyo-no-kata* (a little-known set of forms that preceded and were the inspiration for the Kendo Kata). Planning and preparations were completed, and a very successful seminar was conducted in August 2009.

During a break late in the second day, I asked Randy Manning whether he thought we should inquire about training formally in Ono-ha Itto-ryu. Randy said we should be cautious, but we should at least inquire. I posed the question to Rod, and he responded, "Let's look into it." Rod and Mitsuko were invited to return in December to teach Okabayashi Sensei's versions of the Kendo Kata, and during the interval between seminars they discussed with Okabayashi Sensei what he thought of the idea. The December seminar went equally well and so, with the blessing of Okabayashi Sensei, we commenced training in Aizu Han Kei Ono-ha Itto-ryu Kenjutsu Sokaku-den in February 2010.

While all this was going on, other developments contributed strongly and favorably to the future course of the dojo. On the recommendation of Ellis, we invited internal strength researcher Mike Sigman to teach two seminars (in February 2008 and March 2009) conveying the fundamentals of *ki/kokyu* (energy and breath) with the hope we would be able to integrate these "lost principles" to our aikido.

During the second seminar, Mike made extensive use of a jo to form a physical connection between training partners in various exercises exerting and countering pressure. A student asked how to do such practice when a partner was not available. Mike said that when he goes for a stroll outside, he sometimes imagines a jo placed against his forehead. He said that he "brings his ki up to the jo and walks into the pressure, maintaining the connection." I was sitting directly in front of him as he demonstrated this, walking toward me. As Mike did so, a distinct, one-inch round, red circle—the exact size of the end of a jo—appeared on his forehead. It was astonishing. When I asked him about it afterwards Mike just chuckled and said, "Yeah. I can do that sometimes."

With the study of internal strength well underway, Ellis returned for a final visit in November 2008, at which time he authorized us to teach his approach to aikido.

Mike Sigman during one of his visits to our dojo to teach his approach to internal strength training. Fascinating sessions!

Ironically, the deeper we delved into internal strength training, our previous Yamate-ryu training methodology and its Daito-ryu derived techniques began to make much more sense and offer a greater range of applications than what we were limited to with the experimental aikido curriculum. I'd taken advantage of several chances to train with our old friends from the Yamate-ryu while we were out of the organization and, while attending a September 2010 seminar in Virginia, I was very surprised to learn that I was still considered to be part of the ryu, with my rank intact as originally awarded, and this applied to the rest of our former black-belts, as well. This news meant a great deal to me at the time.

The fact is, some members of the ryu (particularly Josh Freeman) had stood by us, to the extent of contributing significant financial support to our dojo, even after we'd resigned from the Lovret organization. For this reason, along with the fact it was the most enjoyable and complete form of training I'd experienced to that point, I decided in September 2011—

actually ten years to the day from our original resignation—to return to the Yamate-ryu as a direct student of a close friend from the Midwest. The agreement with the then-leadership of the Yamate-ryu and Tenshin-ryu was that we would support Tenshin-ryu events, but our kenjutsu class would continue its focus on the Sokaku-den line of Ono-ha Itto-ryu.

After several years, and leadership changes following the deaths of Lovret Sensei and his immediate successor in 2015, I was informed that Yamate-ryu students in our dojo would not be promoted past *nidan* (second-degree black-belt) unless they also held at least the first license in Tenshin-ryu. This didn't affect several of us who had achieved rank in kenjutsu in the past, but it certainly constrained our junior black-belts. Several of them formed a Tenshin-ryu study group to try to meet the expectation placed on them, but the effort foundered.

I decided that I needed to stop training in Itto-ryu and resume teaching Tenshin-ryu (leadership also having dictated that training in kenjutsu other than Tenshin-ryu would not be permitted).

While visits with the Uhlers gradually became less frequent due to completely understandable circumstances in their lives, we got another surprise in the form of an unexpected guest. I arrived at the dojo one Saturday morning in 2018 while the Itto-ryu class was in progress to discover a gentleman sitting and watching training. He introduced himself as Mark Hague, which meant nothing to me initially, but certainly did by the end of the morning. Mr. Hague was visiting from Japan, where he lived and trained at the Reigakudo—the headquarters dojo of mainline Ono-ha Itto-ryu. He was in the area to settle the purchase of a home located about ten minutes from our dojo. When we understood who he was, we realized several of us owned books written by the headmaster of Ono-ha Itto-ryu that Mr. Hague had translated to English. We asked Mr. Hague whether he might lead a training session at our dojo before returning to Japan, and he readily agreed.

Mr. Hague is a retired military officer and executive for a defense-related corporation, and the home was being purchased for him and his wife to relocate to this area in preparation for his eventual, second retirement. This posed an interesting problem and opportunity for us, in that I did not fancy the idea of "competing" with the highest-ranking Westerner in one of the three top-shelf, authentic koryu schools of kenjutsu (the other two being Yagyu Shinkage-ryu and Katori Shinto-ryu).

Over the next few years, Mr. Hague visited and taught at our dojo more frequently than the Uhlers were able to, and it became apparent to us that continued progress in the Sokaku-den line was unsustainable. This was entirely our fault, not theirs. I was no longer training in Itto-ryu, and no other members of that kenjutsu class were at the time able to travel to the Uhlers in order to train at their dojo in Michigan. Meanwhile, we realized that we could ultimately have Mr. Hague as an instructor to our Itto-ryu kenjutsu class full time, and he agreed to that plan.

As more people in our dojo became exposed to Itto-ryu, and especially after one of the junior Tenshin-ryu black-belts had the opportunity to attend university in Japan and train at the Reigakudo (this was arranged by Mr. Hague), it became evident our two kenjutsu groups should be combined and converted to mainline Ono-ha Itto-ryu. We explained developments to the Uhlers, who were very understanding despite being disappointed, and to the leadership of the Tenshin-ryu.

The Tenshin-ryu leaders were very definitely not understanding and took action, despite my having tried to explain that we were continuing with Yamate-ryu and would support Tenshin-ryu in accordance with the agreement established when we returned to the ryu in 2011. Within two days of my June 2020 correspondence with leadership, I received certified letters declaring us all *hamon* (essentially, excommunicated), stripping all the *yudansha* (black-belts) of their Yamate-ryu/Tenshin-ryu ranks, denying us use of those names for arts, and ordering me to remove all Lovret writings and other materials from any and all media. But what might have been disastrous for our dojo eventually turned out to be the second-best thing that ever happened to us.

My aikijutsu instructor made clear to leadership that he would continue to work with us and, as a *menkyo kaiden* (a license of full transmission) holder, would issue replacement ranks. Later in 2020, his own difficulties with leadership caused my instructor to resign from the Lovret organization and establish his own aiki-budo group.

In mid-2020, I retired following a 40+ year career in federal civil service, having started as a GS-05 and finishing as a GS-14. I worked for the U.S. Navy as a logistician, supervisor, and manager, and careful management of my career path—along with the support of my *very* understanding wife—allowed the personal time needed to operate the dojo and the financial resources to subsidize its operation through much of its existence. Retirement enabled me to start a full-time, professional focus on the dojo.

Meanwhile, the Reigakudo reorganized as the Japanese equivalent of a non-profit corporation and Itten Dojo applied to become an authorized training location. This status was granted in June 2021 by Yabuki Yuji Soke, the 18th headmaster of Ono-ha Itto-ryu following the passing of the 17th Headmaster, Sasamori Takemi Soke, while preparations continued for Hague Sensei to take on teaching kenjutsu at our dojo (which did eventually happen in early 2022).

Itto-ryu does not include iaido (although a separate, somewhat similar type of art is also taught at the Reigakudo). Many members of our dojo, myself very definitely included, enjoy that practice, so I began to consider ways to include iaido in our studies. Our aikijutsu instructor encouraged me to simply take what I knew at the time (roughly 40 different iaido kata from different sources) and run with it but, as might be apparent from previous actions, I'm not a "make-do" kind of person. During a discussion on the topic with longtime dojo member Jevin Orcutt, Jevin said, "Aren't you friends with Suino Sensei? Why don't you ask him to help?"

This turned out to be one of the most profoundly important suggestions ever made within our dojo.

In early 2018 I had posted on Facebook a photo of one of Rosanne's Italian dinners—a pretty routine dinner for her, but spectacular by most other people's measures. Nicklaus Suino was one of the people that commented on the post. I had known of Suino Sensei for decades, had many of his books, and had corresponded with him on several occasions over the years. I responded to his post by inviting him to dinner and using teaching a seminar at our dojo as the "excuse" to make the long trip from Michigan.

Suino Sensei accepted the invitation and, in June of 2018, brought several of his core students from the Japanese Martial Arts Center (JMAC) to Itten Dojo. After the promised feast upon their arrival Friday evening, we spent all day Saturday and then Sunday morning with introductory, overview-type sessions focused on iaido, judo, and *newaza* (ground fighting). It was to prove a watershed weekend, at the end of which I jokingly said to Sensei, "If our current organization ever blows up, I'll probably apply to become JMAC East." Little did I know...

Suino Sensei making introductory remarks at the start of his first visit.

Acting on Jevin's suggestion, I approached Suino Sensei with the possibility of his helping us train in Muso Jikiden Eishin-ryu. Although this effort was initially expected to be just a supplemental practice within our dojo, and although I made clear to him that if he thought a limited program would not be worth his time I would completely understand, Suino Sensei was happy to help.

I will never forget the effect of a short talk Suino Sensei gave the founding members of our fledgling iaido class at the conclusion of the first "official" seminar visit here in September 2020 that launched our formal swordsmanship training with him. Suino Sensei spoke of his personal mission in life and how sharing training in budo is a critical part of his efforts. Those present and listening were transfixed—in a way I'd never witnessed previously in our dojo. Or pretty much anywhere else. During subsequent discussions in the dojo, it became overwhelmingly apparent that those present had been deeply inspired. Not simply to undertake serious training in iaido with Suino Sensei, but to aspire to playing a supportive role in his mission.

And that triggered a transformation—a transformation that has proven to be the best thing that has ever happened to our dojo.

Whether coming out of the pandemic inclined persons interested in training to prefer an art largely based on solo practice, or because of the comprehensive and thoroughly engaging nature of Suino Sensei's approach to the art, the iaido class quickly grew to be the largest group of students within the dojo and a major (or primary) focus for many, including myself. I formally discontinued any training in Ono-ha Itto-ryu in order to focus exclusively on Muso Jikiden Eishin-ryu as my practice of swordsmanship.

Suino Sensei and several of the JMAC seniors after conducting testing for members of our thriving iaido program in 2023.

While our relationship with Suino Sensei and JMAC was growing closer, it dawned on me that the logo used for the dojo, based on a *mon* (crest) still reflecting an association with the Lovret organization, was really no longer appropriate. I decided that a rebranding was in order and asked Suino Sensei whether I might have permission to develop a design incorporating an element of the JMAC logo: the *tsuba* (sword guard) graphic. Once again, I stressed that I would completely understand should he say no. But, once again, he said yes. The new logo for Itten Dojo debuted in September 2021.

I immediately received a message from our aikijutsu instructor, inquiring why I thought this rebranding necessary. I told him that because only one of the three arts in the dojo at that time had any real association with the old, mon-based logo, a more modern and in a sense generic design that could encompass everyone, would better represent the dojo.

Shortly thereafter, I received another message, suggesting that it might be better if we just went our own way. Thoroughly fed up with drama by that point, I agreed.

The only problem was that we had never received the promised, replacement rank certificates, so I found myself running an aikijutsu program without the benefit of tangible credentials. To be sure, rank is not the *most* important thing, but rank is certainly *an* important thing. Would you be comfortable using the services of any professional, a physician or an attorney, that could not produce credentials attesting to their competence? I think not.

So, I reached out to persons I knew and respected that were in a position to help. Miguel Ibarra Sensei of the Yamabushi Jujutsu Aikijutsu Association issued replacement rank for me that exceeded by two *dan* grades the rank I'd held previously—this allowed me to reissue ranks and promotions for my students. Edward Castillo Sensei of the Nihonden Aikibujutsu Senyokai stepped in to endorse my rank and those of my subordinate black-belts, and then Asano Yasuhito Sensei of the Japanese Budo Association issued Japan-based recognition of the ranks. I am forever grateful to these gentlemen for their support and encouragement and I maintain these relationships to this day.

The issue of credentials settled, I now had freedom to consider an alternative path that Suino Sensei had suggested: an exploration of Nihon Jujutsu. To learn more about how that turned out, see "The Art of Letting Go," and "Why Nihon Jujutsu?" later in this book.

I never dreamed that I would be, at this point in my life and fast approaching 70 years of age, pursuing black-belt rank in two new arts, iaido and jujutsu. But here I am. One down (iaido); one to go (jujutsu)—and these ranks are certified by the U.S.-based but international, Shudokan Martial Arts Association. Achieving black-belt is a milestone, but it's just the first step. In fact, that is literally what *shodan*, the Japanese term for first-degree black-belt actually means. First step. The gateway to more serious training.

Our iaido class continues to be the largest group within the dojo and is still growing, to the point additional classes needed to be added to spread-out the attendance. The iaido group by itself is larger than the total enrollment in the dojo in all but a few of its 30+ year existence. The jujutsu class is growing as well, along with the kenjutsu class. The newest addition to the dojo, a *shodo* (calligraphy) class taught by Rie Hashimoto Bailey Sensei, has established an entirely unique aspect to our practice and fully justifies a more descriptive and JMAC-aligned tagline for our logo: Itten Dojo, Japanese Martial Arts and Culture Center.

The future is indeed bright.

2 THE GOLD WATCH

One day, as he was shopping at the local mall, a karate instructor—Ralph Lindquist, the instructor under whose guidance I earned my first black-belt rank, in Isshinryu—was approached and greeted by a gentleman in his early thirties.

"Sensei," the gentleman began, "I don't know if you remember me, but I trained with you for about three years, almost twenty years ago."

As Lindquist Sensei tried to picture the gentleman as a teenager, and thereby jog his memory, the former student extended his left arm, rolled back his sleeve to display a gold Rolex, and said, "I just wanted to say 'thank you' for this watch."

Lindquist Sensei was confused. Although he was only beginning to recognize his former student, the instructor was pretty certain he had never taken enough shots to the head to cause him to forget giving away a gold Rolex.

Noting that his old instructor didn't know what to make of all this, the gentleman offered, "Maybe I'd better explain. As I said, it has been almost 20 years since I studied karate with you. As time passed, I forgot the kata we practiced, and my techniques lost any semblance of power and grace. But one thing you taught me I have never forgotten, even after all these years. I remember taking promotion exams, and the way we were always told, 'Pick a spot on the floor that is advantageous to you, and begin your kata.'

"To this day, I use that teaching. Any time I have gone into a business meeting, made a presentation, been interviewed, or conducted an interview, I have always been careful to pick the spot that is most advantageous to me. Not only in terms of physical location, but with regard to my statements, attitude, and demeanor as well.

"As a direct result, I am now vice-president of the company I work for. This gold watch is a symbol of the lifestyle I enjoy as a result of my success—success I would not have achieved without the lesson you taught me, so long ago."

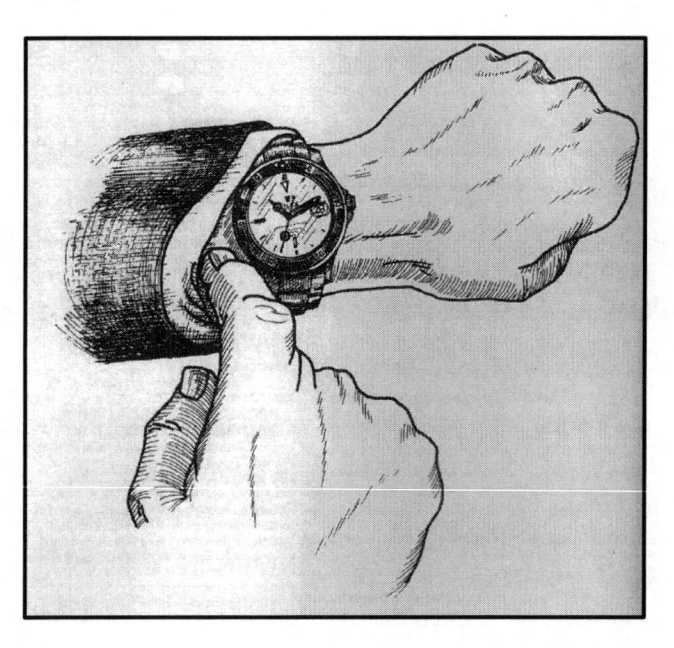

3 FIGHT OR QUIT!

Back in our old karate dojo in the early 1980s, we did a lot of heavy-contact sparring. As already mentioned, multiple members of the dojo went on to compete around the east coast in professional, full-contact kickboxing matches. In the dojo, we wore minimal protective gear and routinely sustained considerable damage on the theory we "would rather take a beating here, than on the street." (Hey, we were good fighters; nobody ever claimed we were intelligent…)

During one intense sparring session, A.J. Boyd was staggered by Dave Bretz's straight right to his head. A.J. went down to hands and knees, trying to regain his wits, as Lindquist Sensei shouted, "Fight or quit, A.J.! Fight or quit!"

A.J. was game to continue the battle but, as he told me later, he just couldn't decide which of the three Dave's standing in front of him he should try to hit.

The above might be somewhat of an extreme example. At the same time, the incident illustrates a decision point all of us reach repeatedly in our lives, and many times in the microcosm of the dojo. The factors leading us to a decision point might be fear, fatigue, conflicting priorities, flagging will, injury, or illness. Regardless of the specifics, we're forced to make the choice to step forward, or step back.

I have always been amazed to see this paradigm play out in one particular aspect of dojo life: the shodan examination. If I look back over my time in karate and aikijutsu/aikido, and count the number of students who reached the point of being qualified and ready to undertake the shodan exam, I find that half the people stepped forward and took the exam. The other half stepped back, and never did. In most of the latter cases, the people quit training completely, rather than take the test. I've even seen two people start the exam, be mentally and spiritually defeated in the course of the ordeal, and quit training on the spot, sometimes after having invested as much as ten years to reach that point.

Any time we step back, let alone quit altogether, I have to believe we emerge from the moment diminished in some critical way.

One karate black-belt candidate, with more than a decade of training and years of experience and sacrifice running a branch dojo, quit his shodan exam only minutes from successful completion. He didn't know how close he was, because Lindquist Sensei had a practice in these tests of telling candidates they were about halfway through, after more than an hour of utterly grueling abuse, when in fact the exams were almost finished.

This particular individual subsequently requested a second chance. The opportunity was granted, and he was required to put in several more months of training. I visited his dojo a number of times to help him prepare. It wasn't going to be easy, but the second time around should have been easier than the first, by virtue of knowing what to expect and being able to train accordingly. But that wasn't how it turned out.

The second exam was held in a grim, unfinished, upper room of an old warehouse. The door to the room was heavy, and had both deadbolts and a sliding bar to secure it. At the appointed time, the black-belt candidate presented himself to the testing panel. Don Denoncourt, the senior member of the panel, twice asked the candidate, "Are you ready?"

Both times the candidate shouted, "Yes, sir!" in response, as though there was nothing in the world that could stop him.

Denoncourt looked the candidate square in the eye and very quietly said, "Good. Lock the door."

And that fellow's knees buckled. Literally. He very nearly fell down. Within five minutes he quit the test, and karate, even though he was physically ready, even though nothing was really going to happen to him that he hadn't already survived. He was defeated by his own imagination.

None of us have an unblemished record in this regard, and we never know what circumstance will bring on the moment of decision.

A.J. Boyd training with Lindquist Sensei when practices were held at the Harrisburg Central Branch YMCA.

I very nearly quit flight instruction early in my training, thereby surrendering a lifelong dream to be a pilot, during an episode of vertigo induced by steep turns. Vertigo kills pilots, and this episode would likely have killed me had I been alone in the plane at the time. Vertigo feels like one's head and limbs are being pulled from one's torso, all in different directions, with a horrible, terrifying sickness radiating from one's gut. The condition is completely disorienting and disabling. Every cell in my body was screaming, "Nothing is worth this!"

The only thing that saved me from quitting was the recollection of the disappointment and, I'm ashamed to admit, the bit of disgust I'd felt just the weekend before, watching another one of those shodan candidates fold in the middle of his test and quit karate. At my flight lesson the day following the vertigo I asked specifically to practice steep turns and had no problems. I soloed shortly thereafter.

But there were other times, in other arenas, I did step back, although the instances I can think of preceded my shodan exam or the incident in the airplane. Even if stepping back from a decision point has diminished us, God willing, we might have the chance later to make up the loss.

None of us have the luxury of knowing in advance which challenges might prove too much. The best we can do is train, facing in the dojo a multitude of small decision points and making the choice in each instance to step forward, hoping that the tempering of a will so forged might provide the wherewithal to make the decisions in life that *really* matter.

Tired tonight, and thinking of skipping practice? Tempted to take it easy during the pushups, and not fight for that final rep? Getting ready to ask if you can receive the technique with a soft roll instead of a breakfall? Looking for a reason to delay taking the next promotion exam? These are all decision points, and can be many small victories, or an accumulation of defeats.

Ultimately, it all comes down to fight, or quit.

4 THE HABIT OF ACHIEVEMENT

Habits are double-edged swords. A huge portion of our routine behaviors are governed by habits rather than conscious decisions—researchers at Duke University assess the portion to be about 40%[1]—and although we sometimes tend to focus on detrimental habits in need of correction, many advantageous behaviors can be cultivated into habits. Even more importantly, a mindset of achievement can be developed by means of physical actions repeated until they become habit.

During admission interviews, many people cite "becoming more self-disciplined" as a major goal in their joining the dojo. That's certainly an excellent reason and an aspect of personal character that can be significantly enhanced through traditional budo. If I haven't already mentioned it in the interview, a candidate raising the topic of self-discipline reminds me to define very clearly an initial challenge to be faced and the means to overcome it. What I'll typically say is something along the lines of:

"I don't know your life story or what you've already been through, but I know from experience that undertaking training in this art will very likely be one of the most difficult things you've ever attempted. If you're serious about this, promise yourself right now that you will complete three months of training before deciding anything whatsoever about it. Three months is the minimum time required to have an informed opinion on the value of the training and what the art can do for you."

Naturally, to get through the interview, almost everyone makes that commitment—and for our part we do everything we can to support the new member through the transition from neophyte to *budoka*. And, most people fulfill the commitment made in the interview. A number, however, just weeks (or even a few classes) into the process, quit, and a lot of those people cite "It's hard" as the reason. I always wonder what, exactly, they thought "one of the most difficult things" meant?

Regardless, what might have been an opportunity to make discipline and achievement an integral component of character instead became a reinforcement of failure.

And that is a dangerous habit to cultivate.

Someone that followed through and fulfilled the "three-month commitment." At four months of iaido training, Mr. Reid looked like this.

James Clear (www.jamesclear.com) is an essayist, and one of his most important pieces of advice for building habits is to start small.

When someone in their admission interview declares, "I've decided to make martial arts my way of life," we know for certain that the person will last no more than three weeks. Even a three-month commitment is a lot, but we're reminded in the *Tao Te Ching* that "A journey of a thousand leagues begins with a single step." New students that break what might be an overwhelming commitment into smaller pieces are most likely to succeed. Instead of thinking, "three months," think "the next practice."

Every practice attended becomes itself a victory, and the foundation of a habit of achievement.

A first-day student learning how to land safely, an early victory helping to establish a habit of achievement.

Being in the dojo counts as the first step. Working to learn the *waza* (techniques), *heiho* (strategies), and applications is the journey. But even in that we encourage new members of the dojo not to worry about trying to learn anything for the first three weeks or so. We're particularly careful to avoid overloading new students with corrections and suggestions that they're not likely to be able to remember, let alone be able to integrate in any useful manner. Instead, we want new members to just have fun, try to move, and get used to the environment of the dojo. Once we see a new member is starting to look comfortable, we begin to point out things that should be remembered and practiced. Persons that adapt to the process of training eventually reach a point at which missing a planned practice is uncomfortable.

The same process can be applied outside the dojo, to any desired habit one wishes to establish. Start small. Count and appreciate the little victories. Most importantly, know that with each successful repetition you are building not just a specific habit, but an overall habit of accomplishing whatever you set out to do.

Note

1. Habits: A Repeat Performance, by David T. Neal, Wendy Wood, and Jeffrey M. Quinn (https://web.archive.org/web/20110526144503/http:/dornsife.usc.edu/wendywood/research/documents/Neal.Wood.Quinn.2006.pdf)

5 "SPIRITUAL" BUDO

Any time I interview a candidate for admission to Itten Dojo, I usually ask what is motivating the individual to seek martial arts training. Some candidates are merely looking for an interesting way to get into better physical condition, while others seek some measure of capacity for self-defense. A few people say, "I don't really know; it's just something I've always wanted to do" (a very good answer, in my opinion, as is, "It looks like fun").

An occasional answer is a desire for spiritual development. This presents a bit of a quandary, because I don't believe the study and practice of martial arts in the West is intrinsically a source of spiritual development in the sense people often assume (or, more properly, have been led to assume, particularly with regard to arts such as aikido). You might find this a surprising revelation, especially considering the title of this book. Don't get me wrong—I do most definitely believe that the various budo are vehicles for personal development in a variety of important respects. I take issue only with some representations of budo as spiritual training.

When I speak of spirit in the context of martial arts, I'm talking about an individual's focused will or intent. At the low end of the spectrum, this might be something as simple as enthusiasm at practice; at the high end it might be ironclad determination to survive an attack or similar, life-threatening circumstance. Spirit as I define it is an aspect of character and something that can be trained.

"Spiritual," in the sense which many prospective martial arts students seem to refer, relates to understanding of oneself and one's place in the universe, insight to the nature of ultimate reality, and the cultivation of moral values. In other words, spiritual in this context addresses topics much more properly, in my opinion, under the purview of religion.

For Ueshiba Morihei, the founder of aikido, there was absolutely no distinction between his personal practice of martial arts and his religion. An ardent adherent of a radical religious movement known as Omoto-kyo (an eclectic mix of Shinto, Taoism, and myth aimed toward achievement of utopia on earth), as well as a personal disciple of its leader, Deguchi Onisaburo, Ueshiba believed aikido to be the product of divine revelation and its physical practice a form of *misogi* (spiritual purification), a means to reconcile Man and Heaven. Aikido training for Ueshiba consisted of daily, spiritually-oriented practice of meditation, prayer, chanting and ritual, *and* time on the mat in the dojo, with both aspects comprising a unified whole. His objective seemed to be becoming in some sense a conduit for effecting the transformation of society worldwide, not just through his example but by means of some direct, personal influence on the underlying structure of the world.

According to researcher Peter Boylan, an overt linkage of martial arts training and religious/spiritual practice is unusual (though not unheard of) even in Japan, outside the writings of Ueshiba and subsequent instructors of aikido. Sure, there have been a number of books over the years attempting to tie budo and Zen, but even cursory review of the available literature pretty quickly demonstrates such linkage—to the extent it exists—is relatively modern. Historically, the samurai were far more interested in Mikkyo, an esoteric form of Buddhism, the practice of which was thought to confer invisibility and other attributes very handy in mortal combat. Note that the samurai were seeking advantage on the battlefield for the benefit of the clan, not individual, spiritual development in the modern sense.

At some point, though, the quest for power in the temporal world was overlaid with at least a veneer of polishing the inner self. Following the unification of Japan at the turn of the seventeenth century and cessation of the state of constant civil warfare that had prevailed for more than 200 years, the practical need for martial training diminished rapidly as most samurai made the transition from warriors to bureaucrats.

Ueshiba Morihei, founder of modern aikido.

Persons wishing to promulgate martial arts had to find reasons to train other than self-preservation, and self-perfection came to be a primary rather than secondary or tertiary objective. At various times over the subsequent 250+ years, the Tokugawa shogunate was forced to mandate training, evidently because so many samurai simply no longer wanted to bother with it. While most people can readily grasp the desirability of acquiring skills directly related to keeping them alive, fewer people are attracted to the concept of arduous training in order to become a better person.

Even today, or more like especially today, the cleverest marketing touts ways to become a better person with no effort whatsoever (and likely implies the reason you're not much to begin with is somebody else's fault). Fortunately for us, and future generations, there has always been a small subset of the world population interested in the study and preservation of traditional martial arts for their own sake.

So, what can the practice of budo accomplish?

I consider the optimal outcome of martial arts training to be the creation of a more capable individual, in as many aspects as possible. The dojo is both a laboratory, a place in which to experiment, discovering one's strengths and weaknesses, as well as forge, a crucible in which to purge fear and temper the body and will. Our training is geared toward physical outcomes of increased fitness, flexibility, and overall health, as well as practical self-defense skills, and spiritual (in my terms) outcomes of enhanced personal discipline and the ability to get a necessary job done when the job is *really* something one doesn't want to have to do (as described in the earlier chapter, "Fight or Quit!"). Mind and body reflect each other, and the greater the degree to which we can improve the functioning of both, the resulting synergism will yield a sum greater than its contributing parts.

As for martial arts training imparting intrinsic moral values, about the best notions I've been able to come up with are:

1. If you fight, you'll likely get hurt even if you win. So, if at all possible, it's better not to get into fights.

2. It's a good idea to be considerate of your training partner, because it's his or her turn, next. In other words, "do unto others..." unless your ukemi is utterly flawless.

3. By being at the dojo, you're not hanging out at the bar, pool hall, or race track (at least not until after practice). On the other hand, depending on the class schedule, you might not be in church, either, so this one is probably a wash.

Beyond that, I just haven't in almost 50 years of training seen any evidence that simply physical martial arts practice effects spiritual improvements of the nature often claimed in books or presented in movies or on television, à la Kwai Chang Caine in *Kung Fu*. In fact, in an unfortunate number of instances, I've observed (and personally had to deal with) just the opposite. Martial arts, being derived from military arts, are, at the core, about the development and exercise of power. And this paradigm is ripe for misuse.

You won't have to look very far in the martial arts world to find utterly contemptible examples of abuse, exploitation, delusion, and grandiose self-inflation. In many cases there is a direct correlation between the number of years of training the perpetrator has under his belt and the egregiousness of the offense. What's worse is that such cases seem most prevalent in the very arts, like aikido, popularly assumed to be the most "spiritual" in nature.

Why this is, I don't know. Perhaps people most perceiving themselves to be lacking in some aspect, are the most susceptible to being taken advantage of, or perhaps hierarchical environments in which some individuals are established as superior in one respect or another to others foster abuse of position.

To be fair, we see these same depredations in religious organizations. The bottom line is all human institutions are inherently corruptible, and can function with any measure of propriety only when all persons involved maintain focus and vigilance and do their best to cleave to an absolute, external standard.

This last is one reason martial arts can fail as spiritual development: while there is an external standard for performance (or even behavior), it is individually derived and not absolute. The founder of an art or subsequent, subordinate instructors can establish standards, but those standards are always subject to revision by other individuals. Only standards external to individuals, things like the Ten Commandments, have any chance of providing a moral compass. (Of course, you don't have to believe in absolutes, in which case I guess you're on your own. Although I concede we, in this world, may not have a completely clear idea of what the absolutes are, I do believe absolutes exist and that it behooves us to try to apprehend the absolutes to the best of our ability.)

The other, primary reason that practice of martial arts doesn't automatically make one more spiritual is the simple fact that perfecting a sword cut, for example, without a conscious intent to use the exercise as a metaphor for honing character, does not yield anything other than a better cut. There's nothing intrinsic to the purely physical practice that might determine to what end that cut is ultimately employed, or that might result in a person becoming saintly. If you want to be able to hit harder, do pushups and practice your punching. If you want to learn how to live, read scripture or philosophy. Pick the tool best suited to the task.

In short, I think anyone wanting to believe the dojo is a substitute for church, or budo an alternative to active and engaged faith, is making a dangerous mistake.

It is certainly true that the dojo, through its constituent members, can provide community, mutual support, and a deep sense of shared purpose. It's also true that the discipline of training can provide meaningful challenge and satisfaction across the course of a lifetime. For some people, this appears to be sufficient. I believe we are better served looking beyond "the course of a lifetime." I believe that everything we do, every thought we think, has spiritual implications and consequences—and I do mean spiritual in the larger sense of soul and a world beyond this. For me, the dojo community and the experience of training are considerably enhanced when viewed within an encompassing framework of faith.

There are more efficient ways to get in shape than practicing martial arts, and far more effective methods to defend oneself. But, all things considered, martial arts do a pretty good job of accomplishing both. Moreover, they're a heck of a lot of fun. And that's the real reason I keep training and instructing. Fortuitously, I think there are grounds to believe at least one of the reasons we are on earth is to appreciate this creation and, where proper, to have a good time. Rather than being a way to gain power in the temporal world, or effect its transformation, the practice of martial arts is to me a way to share, to give back, to express God-given talents in a manner that is, I hope, pleasing to God.

Martial arts may not make us more spiritual, but we can make spiritual the practice of martial arts by what we bring to the practice: reverence for our Creator, love for each other, and joy at the chance to experience it all.

6 MYTHS OF SELF-DEFENSE

Many people seeking martial arts training cite gaining the ability to defend themselves as their primary motivation, while almost everyone seeking training includes "self-defense" capability somewhere in their list of goals. Persons training long-term typically come to recognize a wide range of benefits far exceeding in everyday utility the value of being able to fight and, for them, the ability to defend against an attack is almost a side-effect of their training. Those just starting out and seeking self-defense skills, however, face a bewildering sea of choices in types of arts and methodologies, choices that are further confused by the conflicting claims of different arts to be "the most effective self-defense known to man." It's also true that most inexperienced people focused on self-defense typically harbor serious misperceptions regarding the nature of violence and the types of threats one is realistically most likely to face. These misperceptions can result in persons seeking training to think that marketing claims are actually evidence of effectiveness.

Let's clear up some of the confusion right away: The most effective self-defense known to man is…not being there. After that, if a situation requires physical techniques of combat, all available options are less good. While all martial arts are not equal, virtually every traditional art or modern, unarmed fighting method has been used successfully to defend against an attack in some instance or another. And every art has also failed. The "best" art depends entirely upon the very specific circumstances and conditions in which it's designed or intended to be used. Regardless of the art or method, physical skills are perishable without continuing training.

I rely heavily on the work of Marc MacYoung, Rory Miller, and their colleagues when addressing in my dojo aspects of self-defense beyond the physical, technical repertoire of the arts in which we train. Required reading for my senior students includes MacYoung's *In the Name of Self-Defense* and Miller's *Principles-Based Instruction for Self-Defense (And Maybe Life)*. Both books are highly recommended, and both are available in print and e-book formats. I keep the e-book versions on my phone for quick access, but have print versions to highlight or otherwise mark-up for detailed reference.

To facilitate this discussion, let's drop the term "self-defense" in favor of "personal protection" (which we'll define as the full range of physical and non-physical actions related to self-preservation) and "personal combat" (which we'll define as a circumstance in which an individual is forced to engage, physically, one or more assailants). MacYoung frequently makes the point that self-defense is a legal term, and Miller amplifies that thought, saying, "By claiming self-defense, you are confessing to a crime." Fighting is illegal. Harming another person is illegal. A claim of self-defense is saying, essentially, "Yes, I did harm that person, but my actions were justified because…"

We'll also make the distinction that consensual violence—two or more individuals agreeing to fight over some issue between them—will not be the focus of this essay. Our focus will be personal protection from an assault, a non-consensual, physical attack with injurious or potentially lethal consequences. According to Miller, credible personal protection training should include at least these elements: Ethical and Legal Aspects of Force; Violence Dynamics; Avoidance, Escape and Evasion, De-escalation; Counter Assault; Breaking the Freeze; The Fight Itself; The Aftermath (which can include legal, medical, and/or psychological consequences). Some of these elements are physical, some are academic, and some are a combination of both. The complexity of the non-physical elements is why I insist my students study the works of the real experts in the field rather than pretend that I can adequately cover those elements during regular classes (let alone pretend that I am qualified to do so).

Not all aspects of martial arts training need to be strictly practical or realistic. Some things, especially when you're training for the long-term, might legitimately be done just for fun. The most important thing is to be able to distinguish between practical, fun, and outright fantasy—fantasy being when the purpose, utility, or applicability of an aspect of training is misrepresented, either intentionally or unintentionally, by the instructor. One very common fantasy is the notion that determination and technique will overcome all other factors.

In personal combat, pure luck always plays a huge role, as does physics. Skill and technique can mitigate but not eliminate the advantage of size and strength. The larger person, in addition to being able to generate greater force, can also absorb greater force. A man and woman of the same size and weight are still very unequally matched, due to greatly disparate muscular strength. While just about any martial art or form of training *can* be better than nothing, any training that promotes unrealistic concepts of violence and personal abilities and consequently fosters an unmerited or exaggerated sense of confidence—especially in women—is worse than nothing.

Arts that place heavy emphasis on free-sparring often claim to be the most realistic forms of training. To a degree, that claim has merit, because it is critically important to experience physical contact and unscripted interaction with an opponent, but any form of sparring or grappling is only one aspect of training for personal protection. It's almost ludicrous to claim that competing against a "resisting opponent," in and of itself, in a controlled, sparring scenario, is the most effective preparation for personal combat. In an actual assault, the defender is the person "resisting," and *no* form of sparring—especially in sport-based arts—allows the horrific acts someone assaulting with lethal intent might in reality employ. Or, for that matter, the actions that a defender might need to employ to survive the encounter. Truly "realistic" training is high-risk, and entails very substantial injury rates, or even death rates, as can be seen by losses of military personnel during their training evolutions.

Martial arts are supposed to enhance your life, not make it more difficult to live your life. It seems a bit insane for the average civilian to engage in any form of training that entails frequent and potentially serious injuries in preparation for a hypothetical fight that will likely never happen, and for which the skillset trained could very well be of limited or no utility whatsoever. Doubly insane, when you consider the fact that study of violence dynamics and other, primarily non-physical aspects of personal protection can greatly decrease the likelihood of ever actually needing the physical, combative skills. MacYoung notes, "The good news about recognizing violence dynamics is that the amount of conflict and stress in your everyday life will be greatly reduced."

MacYoung further points out, "Most violence takes place when you're angry, aggressive, or confident." That insight translates to four simple rules:

1) Don't do stupid things.
2) Don't say stupid things.
3) Don't go stupid places.
4) Don't hang with stupid people.

By all means, train in martial arts. If your focus is personal protection, understand that topic is much more extensive than simply the physical techniques of personal combat. Do sufficient research to be able to assess, realistically, the purpose, strengths, and weaknesses of the art you're considering. Nicklaus Suino Sensei, our iaido and jujutsu instructor, offers some great advice: "Choosing the right martial art style and the right dojo can be overwhelming. You can simplify it by asking three questions: Is it safe? Is it systematic? Is it supportive?"

Finding and enrolling in a dojo meeting those criteria will open a pathway to personal transformation that encompasses, yet far exceeds, self-defense.

7 STUPID, STUPID...

We devote considerable effort and time to development of physical skills applicable to self-protection, but all the technique in the world is useless if situational awareness and judgment are lacking at the moment of truth. This point was brought home to me many years ago, under circumstances in which tactical mistakes I made could have resulted in tragedy.

My wife Rosanne is an artist and designer (as you can see by the illustrations in this book). She had recently acquired an account she was very excited about: Two partners were starting a company to market a particular, Philadelphia-style soft pretzel, and Rosanne was hired to design the company logo, product packaging, and all the printed materials and various forms of advertising the new business would require. The account would be her biggest ever.

One late afternoon, I answered the doorbell to find a person I did not recognize standing on our front porch. He introduced himself as the pretzel company junior partner. Rosanne wasn't home at the time, so I invited the man in (this was the first mistake), figuring I would need to write down a message or check for some type of information. Hearing that we had a visitor, my then very young daughter, Erika, trotted partway down the stairs from the second floor to see what was going on.

I'd never met either partner, but my first thought was to be as accommodating as possible. Besides, Rosanne hadn't mentioned any concerns with either partner—nor had she any, prior to this incident.

Surprisingly, though, rather than asking a business-related question, the man asked for cash, saying he was nearly out of gas, but realized he was close to our house. When I inquired why he didn't figure to use a credit card, or hit an ATM, the man said he'd left his wallet at home. At this point, things started to seem a little strange to me, and when I hesitated the guy began to get mildly belligerent. Second mistake: Rather than reassess this person's intent at the first hint of implied threat, I remained focused on the idea that this person was important to Rosanne and I should try to accommodate him.

As the person's requests shifted toward demands, I suggested that I didn't have any cash. Erika, innocent as she was, immediately piped up with, "I do!" (I was headed to the credit union myself the next day, and really didn't have anything much in my wallet at that moment.)

Figuring that in light of Erika's remark the easiest way to conclude the situation would be to provide some cash, I told the fellow to wait a minute and went upstairs to raid Erika's piggy bank. As soon as I rounded the corner, I realized my third—and worst—mistake: Erika was out of sight. I snagged the money and headed back downstairs, with the sick realization that those few moments would have been more than adequate for this guy, this belatedly recognized intruder, to grab my daughter and head out the door.

Between Erika's bank and my wallet, I was able to hand the intruder $20, to which he replied, "Is this all you have?"

Making certain that Erika was well behind me, I told the intruder to get on his way, which, with some measure of grumbling, he did.

As soon as Rosanne returned home, I told her what had transpired and she immediately called the other partner. He apologized profusely, saying that his friend suffered from some particular psychological condition and had a history of doing just this type of thing. The senior partner promised to return the money, which he subsequently did. Rosanne also informed the senior partner that under no circumstances would she again meet or deal in any way with the partner who had "visited" us. As it turned out, the business venture went bust pretty quickly, although Rosanne was at least paid for the logo design and other work she'd accomplished to that point.

So, what were the lessons learned?

The first, and most important, though very disturbing to me, is the demonstration that despite my training I am fully capable of making utterly stupid, tactical mistakes. Self-protection demands a certain level of professional paranoia, the recognition that while everyone might not be out to get you, the few who are aren't going to announce themselves in advance. Take nothing for granted, at any time. Research and apply the situational awareness color codes developed by Colonel Jeff Cooper (see page 50).

Protect the most valuable; forget the rest. I should have been far more worried about Erika's safety than the potential for offending Rosanne's client.

Allow no one personally unknown to you to cross the threshold of your home. Remember that if you even crack the door to someone unknown, the door can be easily kicked completely open and entry forced. Strangers are owed courtesy, as well as assistance when warranted, but not at the expense of making oneself vulnerable to attack.

Samurai kept a naginata hung over the front door, and were never unarmed even when sleeping. If you face a home invasion type incident, inaccessible weapons are worse than useless. (The father of a college friend had firearms loaded and hidden throughout their home. At the time, I thought he was psycho. Now, though, I think he's a shining example of the theory, "Better to have it and not need it, than to need it, and not have it.") Obviously, live weapons in the home must be stored safely and securely, but a variety of means now exist to permit rapid access to weapons while denying any access to unauthorized persons.

Make a plan. Think about possible situations and how threats might be handled. We can't anticipate every contingency, but we can consider at least a few environments in which assaults are most likely and devise general responses. I never again separated myself from a family member in any situation the least bit disturbing. Erika grew up thinking I was overprotective, but that's just the way it was going to be. I was determined that whatever further mistakes I made would be a matter of erring on the side of caution.

And I thank God that I learned this lesson at the cost of nothing more than personal chagrin.

Colonel Cooper's States of Readiness

Condition White: You are essentially unaware of anything going on around you. Maybe you're fatigued, distracted by some worry, or had a bit too much wine with dinner. Regardless of the excuse, you are not ready—for anything.

Condition Yellow: You are alert but calm and relaxed, scanning your surroundings for potential threats. You know who's in front of you, to your sides, and behind you. You don't think anyone will make a hostile move, but you are mentally ready in case something untoward develops. Yellow should be the "default" condition for every martial artist.

Condition Orange: You recognize that something is out of the ordinary, and that the chances for violence are increasing. At this stage you note the positions of all potentially hostile individuals around you, as well as any weapons they may be able to use, in their hands or within their reach. You develop a plan for dealing with the potential hostiles, including identification of escape routes. In addition to being mentally ready, you are physically ready as well.

Condition Red: You are engaged in combat. Someone is assaulting you and you are reacting to the attack and defending yourself. You are taking immediate and decisive action to stop your opponent, or evade and get help.

8 AN ILLUMINATING FOURTH

Harrisburg, the capital city of Pennsylvania, is situated along the Susquehanna River and is unique among cities of similar or larger size in having a completely undeveloped waterfront. For more than four miles, the space between the river and Front Street is a park, with lots of trees, benches, observation stations, picnic tables, exercise equipment, and a walking/biking path. The Susquehanna is an exceptionally scenic river, a mile wide at some points, and just beautiful. For special occasions like art festivals and the like, the downtown section of Front Street is blocked-off to handle crowds of pedestrians and to accommodate food trucks and other vendors. Such is the case for the annual fireworks display on Independence Day. But in 2022, the event turned out to be very different than normal and there were, for me, multiple lessons learned.

The evening of July 4th, my wife and I went to meet with our daughter at her downtown apartment, and then walked to the river and spread a blanket to watch the fireworks display, off the street and near the bank of the river. Originally, I was not planning to go, due to my concerns about large public gatherings in the current national environment, but changed my mind once I knew that our daughter would be going. My wife and I discussed the potential for danger—earlier that day there had been a mass-shooting at a parade in Illinois. Licensed to do so, I went armed (concealed pistol, extra magazine, small knife, flashlight). When we arrived, there were already thousands of people present.

Riverfront Park, looking south. The spot on the right is where we placed our blanket to watch the fireworks.

My daughter had invited a friend to join us, someone who had formerly served as a law enforcement officer in Washington, DC and Harrisburg. While we were standing around, my daughter (knowing that I was armed) asked her friend whether he was also carrying a firearm. He said he wasn't, because he thought there would be too many people in the crowd to allow safe use of the weapon even if it were to be needed.

Lesson One: Assuming you are legally entitled and appropriately trained to carry a firearm, if you have it in your possession, you can always decide not to use it. The opposite is not true.

At about 9:30 p.m., just before the fireworks were to begin, a wave of screaming started a little way to the south of where we were situated and a literal stampede quickly developed, with people shouting, "They're shooting!" The sound of that panicked stampede was unlike anything else I've ever heard. It was a deep, bass roar like the sound of a train approaching, with so many people fleeing up the street.

In the past, I've participated in footraces on Front Street, sometimes with a couple of hundred runners, and nothing ever sounded remotely similar to the thunderous roar of that stampede.

Front Street. The stampede of panicked people surged from the right.

Afterwards, my daughter said her first thought had been, "This can't be happening!" My first thought was, "Well, ****...here we go."

Lesson Two: Regardless of where you live, it can happen there.

Lesson Three: If you consider in advance potential dangers, you may be better prepared to respond in a measured and rational manner.

Lesson Four: Even if you are able to respond rationally, the overwhelming majority of people around you will instead panic, and constitute a significant threat themselves in their mindless flight.

As everything erupted, my daughter's friend instinctively reached for his pistol...but it wasn't there. Regardless, he took charge of my daughter and I stayed with my wife. Partly because of our discussion earlier that day, but mostly because she's just plain good in emergencies, my wife was completely calm.

Lesson Five: Special operations warriors have a saying, "Two is one and one is none." I had never seriously considered carrying a backup firearm in addition to a primary weapon, but now realize that might be relying on hope rather than strategy. The backup is insurance against a mechanical failure in your primary weapon, or running it dry. Or, as this circumstance demonstrated, you might have to arm a companion.

Leaving the blanket, we moved quickly toward the river bank to stay well out of the stampede. We took cover behind a very large tree and paused to try to assess what was actually happening. On the way to the tree, we passed a wide-eyed man squatting beside a picnic table, something that didn't provide either cover or concealment.

Looking across the eastern bank of the river, toward City Island from where the fireworks were launched. This is the picnic bench beside which the gentleman was squatting, utilizing neither cover or concealment. The tree would have been a better choice.

Lesson Six: As addressed in a social media post by Canadian *koryu* and *gendai budo* instructor Reg Sakamoto, "Since the world is getting a little more unhinged let's have a lesson. Cover and concealment. Concealment is anything that hides you from sight, but will not protect you from even small-caliber rounds. For example, bushes. Cover is anything that will protect you from rounds. For example, get down behind an engine block; this will protect you. Not the body of the car, but the engine block."

As soon as things settled down a bit, it was apparent nothing was really happening other than the stampede itself and people being trampled.

The aftermath on the now-deserted street was an apocalyptic scene, with overturned baby strollers, camp chairs and tables, cooler chests, food, and all kinds of other personal belongings, clothing, and electronics abandoned and strewn about. We retrieved our blanket and then regrouped at our daughter's apartment.

We eventually learned that a fight had broken out a block away between two groups of unaccompanied teenagers and that one of the juveniles lit firecrackers, shouted "Gun!" and threw the firecrackers at the other kids. And that got the ball rolling. In the subsequent rush, many children were separated from their parents. We heard little children crying, "I don't want to die, Mommy! I don't want to die!" What a screwed-up country this is getting to be, that mass shootings are now part of average children's consciousness. Other children were completely separated from their parents and were not reunited with their families for many hours.

In the following days, local news reports seemed to be very much downplaying the incident, saying that police stepped in quickly and restored order. Judging by our experience, this was absolutely not the case. I saw no officers in the immediate area, prior to or after the event. It was also reported that there were only minor injuries and that no one required transportation to the hospital. But while we remained at our daughter's apartment there were constant sirens and we could see ambulances coming and going for almost two hours after the event.

Lesson Seven: Ultimately, you are responsible for your own safety. If it's possible in your area, being legally armed may be something you want to consider and make a habit. Understand very clearly, however, that a firearm is not some kind of magic talisman. Even with proper training and practice, a firearm in the hands of the legally armed citizen offers only the chance to not be a victim. That being said, published studies[1] and data collected by the government indicate personal defense with a firearm happens between 2.1 and 2.5 million times per year in this country, and in well over 90% of the instances the weapon does not need to be fired.

Lesson Eight: While traditional martial arts training, depending on the specific art, may or may not be directly applicable to physical self-defense, the mindset developed by traditional training is very definitely an advantage in emergencies.

There are many formal, academic studies of the beneficial effects of martial arts training on health and wellbeing in general, as well as studies specifically examining the benefits of traditional training for developing mental toughness.[2] Over the course of almost 50 years of active training in both empty-hand and weapons-based arts, I've experienced a variety of situations and instructional paradigms I believe to be factors in fostering a survival mindset and calm in the face of danger.

Although training overall should be fun and fulfilling, if it isn't at times at least uncomfortable—or even sometimes more than a bit scary—it's not likely to be training that will produce stronger will. Personal growth does not occur within one's comfort zone. Pushing past perceived limitations and embracing discomfort can be done in a measured and reasonably safe manner. This may be as simple as going to the dojo regardless of not really wanting to, or at a more developed stage, making the decision to enter and then prepping appropriately for a competition in which injury is a realistic possibility.

Awareness of the inherent risk in any given activity, accepting the risk, and conditioning oneself to function within that environment can help instill greater perception and alertness that carries over outside the dojo. Unarmed arts utilizing intense and unscripted sparring and/or grappling excel at creating such an environment.

Traditional judo includes both structured and freestyle practice.

Classical, weapons-based arts even more so, especially those employing "live" weapons, due to the higher level of intrinsic risk in training. The goal is not to be casual about risk in training; just the opposite, in fact. Constant awareness and realistic appreciation of the risk, and then operating effectively in such a way as to manage the risk, is key to optimizing the benefits of training.

Protection of oneself and others is multi-faceted, involving far more than learning a few "self-defense techniques." Taking into account that everyday life entails risks that appear in some respects to be increasing isn't paranoia; it's the kind of realistic assessment and basis for action that should be an outcome of proper martial arts training.

As was made even more clear to me on that Fourth of July.

A typical selection of gear for everyday carry (EDC): A pistol, an extra magazine, a small knife, and a flashlight. Include a mobile phone, as well.

Notes

1. Kleck, G. and Gertz, M. *Armed Resistance to Crime: The Prevalence and Nature of Self-defense with a Gun*. Journal of Criminal Law and Criminology, 1995.
https://www.semanticscholar.org/paper/Armed-resistance-to-crime%3A-the-prevalence-and-of-a-Kleck-Gertz/3a663d85c024baac0d018d7d8bcbca96f19d9964?p2df

2. Minnix, D. *Mental Toughness in the Classical Martial Arts*. Virginia Polytechnic Institute and State University. 2010. https://vtechworks.lib.vt.edu/bitstream/handle/ 10919/26392/Minnix_DW_D_2010.pdf

9 MOMENTUM

While warming up prior to a jujutsu practice, one of the black-belts and I were discussing something—I don't remember exactly what—but he mentioned "momentum" in the context of the dojo collectively and training individually. Subsequent to that evening, the concept of momentum was stuck in my mind. I thought about individual members of the dojo and instances in which their iron-clad intent to move forward, or the dissolution of their intent, made all the difference. And I also thought about the ongoing story of our dojo, how it's survived one black-swan event after another. Some of the events were just random bad luck, while others seemed to be intentional attacks, quite possibly made with the hope of taking us down. The dojo is now in its fourth decade of operation. Still here. And growing. With momentum.

Most people are familiar with Newton's First Law of Motion: A body continues in its state of rest, or in uniform motion in a straight line, unless acted upon by an outside force. In the context of our discussion here, the "force" affecting motion could be mental (as in the case of intent to progress in training, or quit) or physical (as illustrated by various techniques in the arts practiced at our dojo).

I've already talked about interviewing candidates for membership in the dojo, and how one thing always said to them is, "We don't know your life story or what all you might have been through. But we can predict that starting training here will be one of the most difficult things—if not *the* most difficult thing—you've ever attempted. It will take about three months to learn enough to know for certain whether or not this training is for you. Make a commitment to yourself that you will get through a minimum of three months, no matter what."

The persons that made such a commitment to themselves and persevered most often continued training long-term. Some are now black-belts and assistant instructors. Their intent fueled their momentum, and their momentum carried them through the challenge of acclimating to the training.

Others, instead of making a way, made an excuse, and their lack of intent stopped them in their tracks. My personal favorite of such quitting excuses is, "It's hard." To which we usually think to ourselves but don't say out loud, "What part of 'the most difficult thing' did you not understand?"

To be fair, there is a third grouping that can emerge during that three-month period: The individuals that discover a legitimately limiting factor, such as a physical impairment that proves to be too troublesome, those that experience a major change to a work schedule or some other circumstance in their lives, or the individuals that discover they simply do not enjoy the training, at all, and it's not going to get better. In the latter case, fair enough; budo is often an acquired taste, and it's not for everyone.

For those that do acclimate successfully and enjoy the training, even when it's more challenging than enjoyable, training becomes as much something you are as something you do.

It's this aspect of "something you are" that has translated to senior members of the dojo doing whatever it takes to ensure the dojo survives the inevitable hard times. Prior to retirement, I had a fulltime career in federal civil service, so I was never in the least bit dependent on the dojo for income, and I did whatever necessary to keep the dojo running, to the extent of subsidizing the dojo financially. Often far beyond what would have been normal, membership dues in a given year. Fortunately, those kinds of circumstances appear to be relegated to the past, and I am now able to begin recouping the financial investment I've made in the dojo.

Because we are so deeply conscious of what we have all gained through the experience of training together, regardless of the particular art, we don't allow anything to act on our forward motion in a detrimental way. Our momentum has always carried us through to better times.

One of the key aspects of training in budo that makes the endeavor far more than simply learning how to fight is that the techniques and strategies of personal combat can be metaphors for principles and practices applicable across a wide range of situations in life.

Following are two examples.

Aikibujutsu: Shomen-uchi Sutemi-nage

Sutemi means "sacrifice-body," and usually refers to techniques in which *tori* (the person executing the throw) drops to the mat to propel the throw. Even persons not training in martial arts are familiar with the judo technique *tomoe-nage*—against an attempted grab by an attacker, the defender holds on and falls to the ground on their back, simultaneously placing a foot in the attacker's midsection and kicking them up and over.

In this aikibujutsu example, tori lowers her hands to "lure" an attack toward her head. As *uke* (the person receiving the technique) fully commits to his strike, tori drops to the mat, tripping uke. If tori waits as long as possible to move, uke will instinctively follow the target down with his eyes, literally sucking him into the technique. In application, tori would also drop slightly forward, ideally landing a knee on top of uke's lead foot, simultaneously pinning him and cutting his legs out from under him—making this a crippling or even lethal technique, depending on how the attacker falls.

Metaphorically, "If an enemy is rushing toward his own destruction, just get out of his way."

Iaido: Oi-kaze

Oi-kaze means "Tailwind." The waza involves a rapid, multi-step advance to a draw and horizontal cut, and then two more steps to a strong, finishing, vertical cut. Most often in Eishin-ryu iaido, the swordsman stands with knees flexed, even when between forms. Oi-kaze is unusual, in that the swordsman initially stands with legs straightened, and then "releases" the knees to lower his center prior to starting the advance. This is an example of using gravity as an "outside force" to overcome the "body at rest."

Metaphorically, always exploit any circumstance that can enhance the chance of success without requiring additional effort.

Momentum is always in play in our lives. Every significant decision we make sets the course for the future. While most mistakes are recoverable and most missteps correctable, some are not. Whether as individuals or as members of a dojo (or any other organization), be very alert to the direction momentum is carrying you.

10 WHY FORM MATTERS

Traditional Japanese martial arts are demanding endeavors in many respects, but particularly with regard to the emphasis placed on proper form. Obviously, better form can reasonably be expected to yield a better, more effective technique. Some arts take this a step further, positing that the more beautiful the form, the more effective the technique. Beyond an appeal to aesthetic appreciation, this teaching focuses students on an aspect of technique other than "making it work," an aspect that has ramifications beyond the purely physical.

JMAC instructor Dan Holland corrects the entry to a judo-waza.

Persons entering martial arts training sometimes cite a desire to "better integrate mind and body" as a primary motivation. One of our former teachers used to say, "Your mind and body are already as integrated as they're going to get. The state of not being integrated is described in technical terms as...dead."

Everyone pretty much understands this, despite what people sometimes say in their interviews to join the dojo. The understanding is reflected in our awareness that a physical illness can compromise our mental state, while extreme mental focus can sometimes enable individuals to accomplish astonishing physical feats. But there are other aspects to consider, as well.

That the mind can alter the physical structure of the body has been demonstrated in studies of neuroplasticity in the brain. Recent studies have also revealed the extent to which the emotion of grief can trigger fatal coronary events. What we're interested in with regard to martial arts practice, though, is the way in which physical postures or movements can affect the mind.

Composed posture and movement in Ono-ha Itto-ryu kenjutsu practice.

Look on the cover of any yoga magazine and you'll see titles for articles like "Four Postures for a Calmer Spirit." The *kamae* (postures) in martial arts can influence the mind of the person assuming the posture— a neat trick if someone finds themselves in sudden need of courage.

In her article "Benefits Beyond Technique—Posture and Movement in Aikijutsu,"[1] Itten Dojo black-belt Dr. Sarah St. Angelo cites a variety of studies supporting the premise of intentional, physical composure affecting emotions and attitudes:

"A study on meta-cognition—what we think about our thoughts—used confident and doubtful seated postures to evaluate people's confidence in their self-evaluative thoughts. Researchers asked people to adopt a confident or doubtful posture and list several positive and negative attributes of themselves. The strongest effect was seen with the combination of confident posture and thinking about positive attributes: people were most confident in their thoughts when combining confident posture and positive thoughts. Essentially, people were observed to feel the most confident, correct, and effective when combining dominant posture and positive thinking. Training the body for confident (correct) posture and simultaneously training the mind in self-encouragement may have a positive effect on overall well-being."

Itten Dojo assistant instructor Jennifer Bennett displays presence, form, and power in execution of a classic aikibujutsu technique.

Another commonly stated goal of persons joining the dojo is, "I'd like to become more disciplined." What they usually mean is developing stronger willpower—or "stick-to-it-iveness"—across a wider range of life activities, whether related to work, school, career, weight control, or whatever. The fact is, trying to affect a mental process by purely mental means is very difficult. Most people who've never tried to sit still for any length of time would likely think of *zazen* (seated meditation) as a mental discipline. Instead, it's a means of developing mental discipline by practicing physical control of the body and breath. Muso Jikiden Eishin-ryu iaido especially shares this aspect, in that training to impose precise control of the body and breath results directly in enhanced mental discipline.

And that's why form matters.

Note

1. St. Angelo, Sarah. "Benefits Beyond Technique—Posture and Movement in Aikijutsu." *Bugeisha Traditional Martial Artist*, Issue No. 15, January 2023, pp. 70–77.

11 THE POWER OF WORDS

While researching the profile of Suino Sensei that—prior to the death of the publisher, Angel Lemus—was scheduled to be the cover-feature article in the July 2023 issue of *Bugeisha Traditional Martial Artist Magazine*, I listened to an interview of Suino Sensei from August 2022. The podcast was Jason Tracey's *Coffee and Grit* (@roar.nation). During this interview addressing personal development and entrepreneurship, Suino Sensei talked about the relationship between intentionality and happiness:

It's funny—the simplest thing, the "can-opener" for me to change from being miserable to being happy, was when someone asks you how you're doing, say, "Great!" It was salesmanship when I started, right? I'd go to the store and buy a bag of chips and a 7Up and the cashier would go, "How are you today?" And I would say, "I'm doing great!" and they would look up, shocked. Then I'd say, "How are you doing?" They would mumble something and then I'd ask, "What would make that better?" All of a sudden, you're in a conversation or you're helping them and I would leave these silly interactions where I spent $3.47 on a snack and I'd be like, "Well, I feel great." Maybe, just maybe, either they thought I was nuts or they were different, too. But it's proof positive that you can be intentional about happiness. You don't have to wait for it to come to you. You choose it and then everything builds on that. Just how you reply—and it's not like, you know, like faking it till you make it—it's like creating something into existence. Our words are so powerful; what we say, how we react. When we go out into the world and we're energetic and we say we're great...first off, other people pop their heads up and notice.

Suino Sensei is a frequent podcaster, here appearing as one of the regular hosts of the weekly Punch Kick Choke Chat podcast (https://www.punchkickchokechat.com/)

I took this advice to heart and discovered an immediate improvement in my baseline level of happiness and positivity. Of course, I still have concerns and things I'm working on, but the effectiveness of Suino Sensei's approach has proven itself to me.

And that made me think of things Rie Bailey Sensei, our *shodo* (calligraphy) instructor, has said regarding *kotodama*, the Japanese belief that words can affect reality. I'll let Bailey Sensei take it from here…

• • • • •

Japan has a spiritual culture that has been handed down from ancient times and is deeply rooted in the hearts of the Japanese people. We believe that "everything has a SPIRIT in the center." For example, nature itself (such as the sea and mountains), specific animals (that have been deified), and sometimes things (such as tools that have been treated with care). And one aspect of this belief is the spiritual power that dwells inside words, called kotodama (言霊). The *kanji* (character) 言 (*koto*) means "the words," and 霊 (*tama*) means "the spirit" or "soul." Together, these kanji roughly translate as "spirit of the words" and refer to the belief that words contain spiritual power.

Basically, positive words hold positive power, while negative words hold negative power. These powers can influence one's personal environment, the events that are occurring, and even one's state of mind. Therefore, we should be careful with the words we use, because their power will come back to us. Furthermore, this mystical power lies not only in the words themselves, but also in the way and the intonation with which the words are said. Seemingly kind words said with a harmful intent will bear negative energy. It is also believed that calling someone's name out loud can have an impact on that person.

Historically, it is thought that the belief in kotodama dates back to the Nara period (710–794). The term appears in a collection of poems titled *Manyoushu* (万葉集), in which the expression, "the land where kotodama brings bliss," is used to describe Japan.

The roots of kotodama are found in *Shinto* (神道), the Japanese animistic religion. In Shinto, it is believed that not only people, but also animals and all objects, have a soul. In this context, it is not surprising that words are also thought to have a soul. In ancient times, spells and incantations to the *Kami* (神—Shinto divinities) were seen as bearing some divine power especially, if when written, they were spelled a certain way. Shinto priests purposely avoided using words coming from the Chinese language, believing that kotodama power exists only in words originally found in the Japanese language.

Even in modern times, kotodama has been linked with the concept of a "pure" Japanese language, as opposed to the use of "loanwords" from other languages. This belief has political implications that were especially visible during the Second World War. In our current era of globalization, kotodama is sometimes an argument used by people who feel the Japanese language and culture are threatened by Western influences.

Japanese culture stresses the importance of harmony between people, and the general rule is that conflict and negative talk should be avoided as much as possible (at least in public). However, there are certain situations in which the belief in kotodama is very visible.

The first instance is in Japanese weddings, during which guests should be careful to avoid any words that may imply a separation. For example, "to cut," "to break," "to split," "to go back," "to end," etc. The term "opening" is even used to refer to the end of the wedding! In Japan, guests bring money as gifts for the newlyweds and must make sure that the sum they give is not a multiple of two, which may hint at the fact that numbers, just like words, also have power.

Another situation for which there are taboo words is exams. Entrance exams are a significant part of every stage of education for Japanese students, and the matter is taken very seriously. In Japanese, failing an exam is literally said as, "falling at an exam," so the words to avoid come from this lexical field: "to fall," "to slip," "to stumble," etc.

Do words really have spiritual power, and can they affect events? I will let you answer this question according to your own personal beliefs. However, we cannot deny the power words can have on the people around us.

You will probably agree that negative talk, gossip, and hurtful words are less preferable than encouraging, kind words, and constructive conversations. We are the first listeners of our own words. Maybe what we say influences us as much as the people we say these words to.

We live in an era in which we can express ourselves on the internet and be heard by an incredibly broad audience. One of my friends, who is a writer, recently told me about the responsibility she feels when writing her articles. Still, maybe such responsibility should not only be the responsibility of writers and the media, but all citizens. The ancient concept of kotodama reminds us that, under anonymous cover or not, speech, comments, articles, podcasts, videos, and social media postings have power. We should all take responsibility for the words we put out into the world.

When specifically thinking about "What is good kotodama?" I always try to picture an "image" of words. If you could see the shape of words with your own eyes, what color and shape are the words that come out of your own mouth, or the words that come out of someone else's mouth?

Of course, in reality, words are not visible to our eyes.

Even so, the influence of those words will surely leave some kind of feeling when reaching the heart of the other person.

- Is that feeling warm or cold?
- Is it soft and comfortable, or is it thorny and painful?
- Is it transparent or is it turbid?
- Is it shining or is it stagnant?

For me, if I create something, it should be beautiful, comfortable, and gentle; something I would love to share! And if it's such a pleasant thing, I'm sure you'll want to share it with those close to you, too.

Hopefully, the number of people who can create "good spirits of words" will increase on a daily basis, and this world will become a wonderful place.

Note

Rie Hashimoto Bailey was raised in Sendai, Miyagi Prefecture, Japan, but has also lived in Spain, Italy, Washington State, and now Pennsylvania. She speaks Japanese, English, Spanish, and Italian, and is a professional international travel coordinator. Bailey Sensei is ranked 7th-dan in the Tonan school of shodo, is a Reiki master and teacher, and an alternative medicine practitioner.

12 THE FROG IN A WELL

My all-time favorite Japanese proverb:

井の中の蛙大海を知らず
I no naka no kawazu, taikai wo shirazu
"The frog in a well knows nothing of the great sea."

This proverb, brushed by a 13-year-old Miyamoto Musashi over top of the inscription on the *kanban* (dojo signboard) of a local kenjutsu instructor, resulted in the confrontation during which Musashi killed his first opponent. The signboard had declared that Arima-ryu, the style created by the instructor, exceeded anything previously seen in the world. Evidently, the style fell a bit short of that mark.

Having confidence in the art you're studying, or confidence in the quality of what you know, is one thing. But that confidence has to be balanced by recognition that there is always more to learn, more to know, and that no matter where you are in your budo journey, there will always be those that already have more of what you want. Thankfully! Imagine how sad it would be to know all there is, to have nothing more toward which to strive? Or, worse, knowing there is more but having no one that could assist you on your journey?

Ralph Lindquist, the Isshinryu karate instructor under whom the Wolfes and Starners originally trained, had a saying: "The next stage after ripe is rotten." It was his admonition to avoid any notion of having arrived at the summit of one's training, an admonition that complements very nicely the warning to avoid being that frog in a well.

Both the Japanese proverb and Lindquist Sensei's saying were called to mind as I reflected on the things our dojo experienced over the past several years.

In presenting the history of the dojo in the first chapter of this book, I described how, in mid-2020, in consequence of the desire of the members of our (at that time) two, separate kenjutsu classes to merge and focus on mainline Ono-ha Itto-ryu, we found ourselves on the outside of the kenjutsu/aikijutsu organization to which we had belonged and faced with the necessity of completely restructuring our dojo. While trying to determine the best course, several of us wanted to maintain a practice of iaido (solo forms with the Japanese katana) in addition to kenjutsu.

I wasn't sure how to do that, until Jevin Orcutt suggested I talk to Suino Sensei about it. I had been acquainted with Suino Sensei for decades and just two years previously he and several of the senior members of his Japanese Martial Arts Center had visited our dojo for a weekend of training, just for fun.

When I mentioned the plan to another, now former, instructor, his response was, "You already know everything you need to know about iaido. Just teach what you know."

The problem with that, in addition to the comment being the epitome of "frog in a well" thinking, is that I've never been content to just settle.

For anything. Especially with regard to training, I want the best, not just for myself, but for the members of Itten Dojo. That attitude is what led to the founding of Itten Dojo in the first place.

Fortunately, Suino Sensei responded positively to my inquiring whether he would consider working with us, and we very quickly had a plan. Although originally intended as a supplemental study, iaido within our dojo took off, to the extent that the iaido class quickly became the largest component within the dojo. Even more importantly, iaido has been a very constant reminder of just how much I don't know. Not a week goes by without some significant insight gained through this training, whether it be during training in-person with Suino Sensei, during an online training session, reading one of his books or articles, or reviewing one of his instructional videos. I've trained a very long time in several schools of Japanese swordsmanship, but I've never learned as much about the art, as rapidly, as I'm learning now.

Suino Sensei instructing, during a 2023 visit to Itten Dojo.

Interestingly, Suino Sensei is himself a student of several other arts. Relatively recently, he returned to the formal study of karate under the guidance of a superb (and surprisingly young) Japanese sensei. Likewise, Edward Castillo Sensei, another close friend and mentor, while continuing to experiment and develop the line of aikibujutsu he inherited, trains as a student of kenjutsu under Asano Yasuhito Sensei in Japan.

And Asano Sensei has a sensei…

These gentlemen exemplify the exact opposite of "frog in a well" thinking. Rather than resting on their laurels and "just teaching what they know," they're stepping past the boundaries of familiarity and training as students themselves, a process that inevitably brings fresh insights likely to enrich their own lives and invigorate the lessons they provide their own students.

If you're not currently training, but are seeking instruction, I would make a suggestion. When visiting a potential dojo, rather than asking about the ranks or the competition history of the head instructor, ask who he currently trains with.

13 WHY IAIDO?

In the June 2018 issue of the Itten Dojo journal, *Sword and Spirit*, I presented an essay titled "21st Century Kenjutsu," which discussed the significant and wide range of practical benefits to be derived by training in the seemingly anachronistic, even obsolete art of combative Japanese swordsmanship. Now that our kenjutsu class is one of the very few groups in the world authorized by the *Reigakudo*, the headquarters dojo in Tokyo, to offer authentic training in Ono-ha Itto-ryu, the potential benefits to be gained are even greater. But, what about iaido, the other *koryu* (old-style) form of Japanese swordsmanship practiced at Itten Dojo? Compared to kenjutsu, the benefits are if anything a bit less obvious. The reality, though, is the benefits of iaido are equally broad and deep—similar in some ways and different in others, but with unique attributes that can make iaido an ideal endeavor for persons that might otherwise never have considered training in martial arts.

Our iaido class trains in Muso Jikiden Eishin-ryu, an almost 450-year-old tradition and the source of most extant styles of iaido. We're especially fortunate to be training under the guidance of Suino Sensei. Suino Sensei was a personal student of Yamaguchi Katsuo, considered by many to be the greatest swordsman of his generation. While living in Japan and training daily with Yamaguchi Sensei, Suino Sensei was All-Tokyo Champion for four consecutive years between 1989 and 1992, competing against hundreds of Japanese in their native art of iaido. He's written four books on Japanese martial arts and consults internationally on strategies for personal and professional growth using the principles of swordsmanship. Even more importantly from our perspective, Suino Sensei and his senior assistants at JMAC have developed a proprietary method of training in this ancient art that bestows on its practitioners challenges, opportunities, and insights that guarantee, with proper attitude and dedication, a transformative experience.

A young Nicklaus Suino, training in iaido at the dojo located in the home of Yamaguchi Sensei.

For those not familiar with iaido, this art of drawing the Japanese sword to an immediate, defensive technique, began as a subset of kenjutsu. The solo forms being practiced are codified answers to the problem of surprise attacks, answers originally developed by Japanese warriors that experienced (and survived) such assaults. According to Kim Taylor, a prominent Canadian instructor of iaido, kenjutsu, and jodo, the term "iai" is derived from the phrase, *"tsune ni itte kyu ni awasu."* The meaning of this phrase is:

"Always, whatever you are doing, whether sleeping, walking, running, or sitting *(tsune ni)*" and "wherever you are *(itte, iru)*" you must "be ready or be prepared to recreate harmony or balance *(awasu)*." *Iai* comes from *itte* and *awasu* and is a short way of remembering this phrase.[1]

It should be apparent that, once swords are drawn, to "recreate harmony or balance" is most likely a matter of cutting down an enemy. And, in fact, all but one of the more than 70 forms in Eishin-ryu involve a lethal resolution.[2] But not necessarily immediately. In many of the forms the draw is executed in such a way as to provide the "attacker" a moment to reconsider, while still assuring the ultimate victory of the "defender."

This philosophical aspect is a reflection of the concept of *katsujin-no-ken* (the sword that gives life) and distinguishes iaido from schools of iaijutsu in which the overriding goal typically is putting steel into an enemy as quickly as possible. Suino Sensei elaborates on the philosophical aspect of iaido:

In Japanese swordsmanship our highest goal is expressed in the phrase saya no uchi or saya no uchi no kachi, which means "victory with the sword still in the scabbard." It is an exhortation to the swordsperson to recognize that physical combat is a last resort, and a reminder that a master strategist will find a way to win without fighting.[3]

The philosophical foundation of iaido is one of the most important considerations for individuals who would like to train in a martial art but have no particular interest in overtly combative practice or tournament-style competitions. The philosophy manifests as well in the *reishiki*, the ceremonial etiquette that is a very major focus of training. Reishiki reinforces the notion that there is a correct way to do almost anything, ranging from physical techniques to social interactions. Focusing on and acting in accordance with "the correct way" is a discipline that will reliably facilitate the polishing of one's character.

It is in the *kihon*, the physical fundamentals of Suino Sensei's approach to iaido, that the strengths of the JMAC methodology become most apparent. Not part of the traditional curriculum, Suino Sensei's stepping and bokken drills nonetheless are built from very specific, physical components of heritage Eishin-ryu, distilled and amplified to illuminate for the sword student proper posture, body structure, generation and application of power, and correct form—and provide the tools/exercises to enable the student to achieve those ideals. An example of just one of the drills, "Long Stance Stepping," was presented in the September 2021 issue of *Sword and Spirit*.

Iaigoshi, the "Long Stance," is a fundamental posture in Eishin-ryu iaido, and is extensively trained in the stepping and bokken drills.

    The stepping drills in particular have proven to hold very personal significance for me. Early in 2021, I suffered a torn medial meniscus in my left knee (the injury was not from iaido, by the way). The tear was at the root of the meniscus which, I was informed, is about the worst place for such an injury. I undertook the recommended physical therapy but it quickly became apparent that surgical repair would be required. The options were an extensive procedure that would have wired everything back into position but would have entailed a more than six-month recovery and promised only mixed results at best, or an arthroscopic procedure that would clean things up and (hopefully) be good enough. I chose the latter option. Two weeks post-surgery, I was told I could plan to do, within reason, whatever was comfortable. Very quickly, I resumed doing the stepping and bokken drills, at least in a limited range of motion.

    At the six-week, follow-up appointment with my surgeon, we discussed whether I should start another round of physical therapy. I showed her what I was able to do, in both range of motion and strength, and her reaction was, "Wow. You're already way ahead of the game. Just keep doing what you're doing." Looking back, I think the "Seiza: Stepping In and Out" drill—sitting down, Japanese-style, and then rising again in a strictly-defined sequence—contributed the most toward my recovery. Detailed instructions can be found in Suino Sensei's *Practice*

Drills for Japanese Swordsmanship.[4] It wasn't my favorite drill prior to my injury, but now I love it. It's amazing how delightful an uncomfortable and physically challenging exercise can be, when one is simply grateful to be able to do it!

Crossing the mat in the "Seiza: Stepping In and Out" drill builds strength and coordination.

The solo bokken drills take many of the stepping sequences and add the wooden sword. Now, in addition to having to deal with configuration of the body, students must incorporate all the aspects that define proper cutting, as well as a significant element of timing.

The solo bokken drills take a variety of the stepping drills, add a wooden sword, and teach the fundamentals of swordsmanship.

The solo drills lay the foundation for the paired bokken drills, which in turn lay the foundation for eventual bokken free-sparring, something that is very unusual to see in schools of iaido, but that ultimately takes training from the realm of pretend to actual application and results in the creation of much more complete swordsmen and swordswomen.

Not formal techniques from any particular system, the two-person bokken drills introduce basics of distancing, timing, angles, and extension.

Suino Sensei describes the inspiration for and development of the stepping and bokken drills:

When I returned to the U.S. after living and training in Japan, I quickly learned how difficult it was for iaido beginners to do even simple forms well. Faced with learning the patterns, building the muscles, and developing fine motor control, many struggled. So, I reflected on my days of training with Yamaguchi Sensei. He would reduce movements to simple components, work with me to understand how to do them with structure first, finesse second, then show me how to incorporate them into the forms. The stepping and bokken drills are core thematic movements of Eishin-Ryu iaido, repeated in a rational manner, to simplify and speed up learning.

Another of the unique and overwhelmingly important exercises in the JMAC repertoire is the "Big Five," an inexhaustible exploration of the major components of many Eishin-ryu *waza* (techniques—in Eishin-ryu, solo forms are referred to as waza rather than kata). The term "inexhaustible" applies because although the drill is relatively simple in its earliest iteration, as the student becomes more experienced and layers of complexity are introduced, the elements demanding exacting attention to detail multiply rapidly. The exercise focuses on the following five components, and is practiced standing in place, with the feet about shoulder-width, and the knees flexed:

1. *Nukitsuke* (Drawing the sword to a horizontal cut)
2. *Furikaburi* (Swinging the sword up, through a defensive transition, in preparation to cut)
3. *Kiri-oroshi* (A vertical cut, considered the most difficult cut to execute entirely properly)
4. *O-chiburi* (Symbolically removing blood from the blade)
5. *Noto* (Sheathing the sword)

Time spent in front of a mirror, practicing the "Big Five," pays significant dividends.

Initially, the exercise is performed with attention to the fundamental movements, then with fundamental movements and the proper sequencing of breathing (generally, inhaling on "opening" movements; exhaling on "closing" movements), and then with fundamental movements, proper breathing, and appropriate cadencing of the movements. Suino Sensei emphasizes that there are many layers of focus beyond those basic three:

Yamaguchi Sensei liked to say that each of the five movements had five components, each of those components had five aspects, and on and on to drive you ever deeper into the learning process. He emphasized starting and ending with the basics, and that's what I do as well, but when a challenge presents itself—such as how to smooth out the transition from sheathed sword to drawn sword—I recommend approaching with many different emphases. There's no substitute for daily, concentrated practice!

On Suino Sensei's *Permission* website, there's an excellent (and very modestly priced) video addressing the Big Five. The video was shot using Zoom, so the image is backwards, but I've found this to be a real asset: You can train along with the video and it's like looking in the mirror, making imitating and correcting much easier. Access this and many other instructional videos addressing a wide range of martial arts and personal development topics at https://permission.thinkific.com.

The largest portion of training time is devoted to the sets of waza that comprise the overall, formal curriculum of Eishin-ryu. Suino Sensei's *The Art of Japanese Swordsmanship*[5] is the master-text describing the solo forms, and there are multiple reference videos available on the *Permission* website. Historically, the creation of the various sets is known, both in terms of the dates of creation and the persons responsible, in a range from the late 1500s to early 1900s.

Even at the introductory levels, I have discovered the solo forms in the line of Eishin-ryu we're privileged to study with Suino Sensei are far more nuanced and richer than any other tradition of iaido I (along with several other senior members of Itten Dojo) have experienced. Our experience has been gained over decades and has included training in a modern, classically-styled system of kenjutsu and iaijutsu, in a different line of Eishin-ryu, and in the All-Japan Kendo Federation standard iaido forms.

The Eishin-ryu waza are pure fun. The forms are not easy, and can in fact be pretty frustrating, but for anyone able to enjoy the journey instead of focusing on the destination, training is a joy. There's nothing quite like hitting a just-right cut and listening to the searing slice of the blade through the air. That sound, or the lack thereof, is an immediate source of feedback during every moment of training. Because of the ready availability of such feedback, combined with the way focus on maintaining a proper *tenouchi* (the grip on the hilt of the sword) tends to help tie things together, I've noticed beginners training in the Suino methodology are developing key aspects of proper form far more quickly than I've seen to be the case in other forms of swordsmanship we've studied.

Chudan-gamae, the "mid-level guard," a poised and ready position.

Suino Sensei agrees:

Our iaido training is highly focused on structure; our teaching approach emphasizes constant repetition of core thematic movements. That's why students develop form and balance relatively quickly, and why those who train passionately over the long term become really solid swordspersons.

There are still more components to training within the JMAC approach to iaido, including the traditional sets of paired, combative kata—*Tachiuchi no Kurai* and *Tsumeai no Kurai*—along with requirements for *tameshigiri* (test-cutting). Tameshigiri involves the use of a *shinken*, a "live," sharpened steel katana to cut targets consisting of rolled, straw mats. The mats are soaked overnight and then drained and bound, and provide a resistance closely similar to flesh.

Rolling mats for a session of tameshigiri in the field behind the dojo.

Given the mystique associated with Japanese swords, many people might assume cutting a straw mat to be beyond simple, but such is absolutely not the case. Japanese swords *are* incredibly strong—in very exact planes and lines. I've seen someone transform a katana into an "L-shaped" club, just by slightly (and sloppily) altering the trajectory of his cut while midway through the target.

Cutting properly and effectively, without damaging a blade, is a very demanding and highly technical endeavor, and quickly separates the swordsmen and women from the wannabes. Suino Sensei's emphasis on tameshigiri is another factor ensuring JMAC and Itten Dojo iaido students are based in reality rather than fantasy. Note as well that, after achieving black-belt rank, students are permitted to use shinken in their own practice of the solo waza.

• • • • •

I hope this overview has provided you some insights to the way we train in iaido. Now I want to address the "Why?" by sharing my enthusiasm for the Suino/JMAC methodology and listing the very personal benefits I have already experienced. Bear in mind, please, that I have at this point almost 50 years of intense and in-depth training in both *gendai* (modern) and koryu budo, and multiple black-belts. If training in this methodology can be so fresh and empowering for me, with my background, just imagine what it can mean for you.

JMAC assistant instructors demonstrating bokken fencing at the 2023 International Iaido Training Camp in Kitchener, Ontario. Photo courtesy of Chris Hanson of Karate Unity (https://www.youtube.com/@KarateUnity).

Let's start with the more purely physical lessons. Soon after I'd become comfortable with the basic patterns of the stepping drills, I realized that the exercises are an incredible laboratory for researching the best means of generating and applying power. At every single practice, I learn something new or refine an existing understanding of how to compose my body for optimal effectiveness, and I take those lessons-learned out of the dojo, and into everyday life.

Posture deserves constant attention, and Suino Sensei's concept of "bow and arrow upper body" has implications that extend far beyond cutting with a sword. Normal walking and moving, which for me have long been a way of all-the-time training, have been illuminated by the stepping drills. I've become more alert to and able to control increasingly subtle aspects of the generation and application of power, through skeletal alignment, sequencing the exact areas of the feet contacting the mat, how that contact is used, what is for me an entirely new way of looking at hip power, and the constantly varying weighting of the feet. The things I'm learning are also enabling me to punch and kick even more powerfully than I'd previously been able to strike.

The mental benefits of iaido training are also proving to be quite significant. Because training is so substantially a process of configuring and controlling the body in accordance with an idealized form that can be pursued but never fully attained, the mental and intellectual involvement required for progress is huge. Development within the art requires a very high level of self-reflection, analysis, and honesty—essentially the ability to identify, consider, and correct what might be substantial or very subtle divergences from the idealized form.

JMAC assistant instructor Nick Miller leads training during a seminar at Itten Dojo.

Additionally, in iaido practice, the imaginary "attackers" must be visualized in great detail. Otherwise, practice becomes little more than going through the motions, or simply dance. Visualizing the opponents during kata practice was not something at which I was successful in previous arts, but is an interesting phenomenon I am increasingly able to experience. All of the mental demands of iaido practice are, in a very literal sense, exercise for the brain, something that will pay dividends to any students, but most especially to those practitioners (like me) who are older.

The most surprising consequence, to me, of the unique physical and mental attributes of iaido practice has been the spiritual effects of training.

Most surprising, because the same effect has been noted by several very different members of our iaido class, ranging in experience from a few months to many decades and in age from 15 to 65. After an iaido practice, many of us have noticed that we feel as though we've worked out, but rather than being charged up we feel particularly calm and focused. It's a very different feeling than I've experienced in any other forms of martial arts training—it's an especially pleasant sensation—and it's a feeling that persists long after the actual practice session.

Suino Sensei notes:

Yamaguchi Sensei wrote: "The secret to iaido is a calm spirit. With a tranquil heart you put your hand on the hilt of your sword—in a split second your hand moves to cut down the opponent and re-sheath the sword—then return to your composed mind."

Good breathing paired with the unfolding of a well-performed iaido waza has a settling effect on the nervous system. Good posture reinforces relaxed alertness. Expressing power efficiently with the mind engaged develops gravitas. Being fully present in the moment creates a lightness that belies the effort needed to move and cut well. In 54 years of martial arts training, I've never experienced anything that brings all these qualities together in such a magical way.

From left, the author, Suino Sensei, and Itten Dojo co-founder and assistant instructor Alan Starner, during a visit to JMAC.

Notes

1. Kim Taylor, "An Interview with Japanese Sword Instructor Haruna Matsuo," *Journal of Asian Martial Arts*, Vol. 5 No. 2, 1996. Reprinted in *The Sword in Japanese Martial Traditions* (Via Media Publishing, 2017).

2. Nicklaus Suino, "How to Watch Iaido," *Journal of Asian Martial Arts*, Vol. 3 No. 3, 1994. Reprinted in *The Sword in Japanese Martial Traditions* (Via Media Publishing, 2017).

3. Nicklaus Suino, *Strategy in Japanese Swordsmanship* (Boston: Weatherhill, 2007).

4. Nicklaus Suino, *Practice Drills for Japanese Swordsmanship* (Boulder: Weatherhill, 1995).

5. Nicklaus Suino, *The Art of Japanese Swordsmanship* (Boston: Weatherhill, 1994).

14 THE ART OF LETTING GO

There is, supposedly, a classical strategy in kenjutsu known as *hanashi-no-heiho*—to discontinue a strategy that is not effective and try something else. I say "supposedly," because I've only ever seen this discussed in one book, in English, and at that a book that does not cite sources. According to Rie Hashimoto Bailey Sensei, our *shodo* (calligraphy) instructor and resident expert in Japanese language, history, and culture, even using Japanese search engines and websites she was unable to find confirmation of this claim. So, we'll take another route to approach the topic.

I eventually found the source for a quote I referenced in an essay some time ago, but couldn't find at the time I was writing. I had thought, incorrectly, that the line might have come from *The Little Prince* (but I did at least get the French part right). Charles Du Bos was a late-19th/early-20th century French essayist and literary critic. His quote that so deeply resonates with me is:

> *"The important thing is this: To be able at any moment to sacrifice what we are for what we could become."*

Multiple times in my personal life I've reflected on this quote when facing a transition that seemed at first daunting, disadvantageous, or even distressing. And I've had as many, or more, opportunities to consider "letting go" over the 30+ year history of our dojo.

The senior members of Itten Dojo are intensely serious about training, and the juniors are typically well on their way to becoming so. Obviously, we enjoy what we do and have a lot of fun doing it, but at no time are we casual about our studies. At a number of critical junctures, we've had to completely reinvent the dojo, when circumstances—sometimes chosen, sometimes not—dictated a change in the teachers we work with and/or the arts we study. The most important lesson we've learned through these events is that the members of the dojo training together and supporting each other is more important than the specific art(s) we're training in. As one of my old karate instructors used to say, "It is the doing and the sharing of the doing that is the essence and true value."

That being said, when the remaking of the dojo results in new relationships that are manifestly healthier, and arts to train in that are far more valuable in every way, it's a huge win for everyone.

We're going through another such transition now.

I've described how, in consequence of events in mid-2020, I first approached Suino Sensei to inquire about training with him in iaido. Even though I presented the request in terms of our training in iaido being just a supplement to the other arts in our dojo, Suino Sensei readily agreed. Little did I know that iaido would rapidly become the primary art practiced at our dojo, with the largest number of students involved—more than 60% of the overall membership—and such a passion for me that I would give up training in kenjutsu completely. The trend with iaido seems to have established a precedent when training with Suino Sensei.

The mid-2020 event led eventually to our being cut-off from all senior-level instructors in our legacy art of aikijutsu. Initially, our instructor cadre focused on crafting our independent approach to the art. Our motto became, "If it's baroque, we'll fix it." As part of process, we scheduled a jujutsu session with Suino Sensei during one of his weekend visits here. At the end of that session, Amber Cathey—then a brown-belt—and Dan Holland Sensei demonstrated Kihon Kata II from Nihon Jujutsu. Watching Ms. Cathey toss Holland Sensei my first thought was, "Oh, man, I wish the women black-belts were here to see this."

Followed quickly by, "Oh, man, I am *glad* they're not here to see this." Because their logical question would be, "Why aren't we doing that?" I only regret that I do not have video of that demonstration.

Amber Cathey Sensei demonstrating a Nihon Jujutsu kata during a 2023 seminar at Itten Dojo.

Discussing the matter further with Suino Sensei, it was decided we should learn Kihon Kata I from Nihon Jujutsu, to facilitate Sensei working with us in his "real-time" self-defense applications. This seemed like a reasonable approach, again with the intent to just supplement what we were doing with aikijutsu. But, as had been the case with iaido, original intent went straight out the window when we experienced our first real exposure to Nihon Jujutsu.

Alan Starner and I were at JMAC for the introduction to Kihon Kata I, and the experience was eye-opening, to say the least. Our legacy practice of aikijutsu was in a derivative of Daito-ryu aikijujutsu, and while a lot of fun to practice, the techniques tended to rely on intricate manipulations—which is to say, fine motor skills—that are the first thing to evaporate under stress. It was often demonstrated that these fine manipulations were critically important factors that had to be present in order for a technique to work. And that was true, within the context of the intricate applications. Consequently, in the first several years of training the emphasis was on highly collaborative practice. Students were literally told, "At this point, you won't be able to make the technique 'work,' but if you focus on working with your training partner to create an ideal representation of the technique, you'll learn the requisite body skills and eventually be able to execute the technique against an actual opponent."

The first technique in Kihon Kata I is *Ude Hineri Nage* ("Forearm Twisting Throw"), analogous to *Kote-mawashi* ("Turning the Wrist," sankyo for the aikido folks). Right off the bat, Mr. Starner and I realized that Ude Hineri Nage violated several of those "critically important factors" that supposedly had to be present for Kote-mawashi to work, and then had the temerity to work better. A whole lot better. As in, it doesn't matter what *uke* (the person on the other side of the technique) is doing, if the technique is reasonably in the ballpark uke is going down, better.

And then the same blasted thing happened with the next technique, *Uchi Tenkai Nage* ("Inside Turning Throw"), analogous to *Shiho-nage* ("Four-direction Throw"). Mechanically much simpler and more intuitive to apply and devastatingly more effective.

And the same with *Kote Gaeshi Nage* ("Returning the Wrist Throw"), analogous to *Kote-gaeshi*.

And with *Ude Kujiki Osae* ("Elbow Wrenching Takedown"), analogous to *Ude-osae* ("Controlling the Forearm").

And with *Ude Kakae Nage* ("Elbow Locking Throw"), analogous to *Zetsumyo*.

At that point of the session I was thinking, "Well, $%* ^ !!! We have a problem." Five of the eight *waza* (techniques) in the kata had direct analogies in our legacy practice, but the Nihon Jujutsu versions were clearly superior.

As we've seen more of Nihon Jujutsu the experience has been entirely consistent. Yet another example is the Nihon Jujutsu applications of *Kote-gatame*, a wrist-lock called *Kote-maki* in our legacy practice (*nikyo* in aikido). In every instance, the Nihon Jujutsu versions are easier to achieve and provide faster, more complete control.

So, we're now well into our transition to Nihon Jujutsu. Initially, we thought we might retain some aspects of our legacy practice that we found useful or that we particularly enjoyed, but that thought pretty much went out the window the further into Nihon Jujutsu we've trained. The advantages to this path are enormous, and include the fact the body mechanics are highly complementary to our iaido training—in fact, we're finding those two arts to be mutually reinforcing.

The best part is I no longer have to tell new students they won't yet really be able to do something. It's become, "Here. Do it this way." And, BOOM!

15 WHY NIHON JUJUTSU?

In the previous chapter I wrote about my experience during a visit to JMAC to learn Kihon Kata I from Nihon Jujutsu so that Suino Sensei could work with us in his "real-time self-defense" applications. Kihon Kata I includes several techniques that are closely analogous to waza in our legacy style of aikijutsu. Analogous, but clearly superior, while breaking a variety of supposed rules we'd been taught *must* be followed for the waza to work. The Nihon Jujutsu versions of the techniques worked far more efficiently and effectively, even against a resisting training partner. By the end of that initial session of jujutsu at JMAC, my previous intention to build a curriculum on a foundation of our legacy art...died.

Now that we are well into the transition from our former practice of aikijutsu to Nihon Jujutsu, under the direct guidance of Suino Sensei and with the support of John Gage Sensei (the current leader of Nihon Jujutsu), I'd like to highlight some of the things I've learned in these early stages of training that will help explain my fascination with and heartfelt "conversion" to this art. Please note that what follows are my personal perceptions that, while based on my decades of training in related arts, are nonetheless potentially compromised by my limited experience at this point in Nihon Jujutsu. If I'm off base in anything I say, I trust Suino Sensei will correct me.

As described on the homepage of the Nihon Jujutsu website (https://www.nihonjujutsu.com):

Nihon Jujutsu is a modern Japanese martial art that focuses on practical, efficient techniques as originally found in both ancient and contemporary martial arts. Its principles and techniques derive from Japanese unarmed combat and self-defense techniques from pre-1945 judo and aikibujutsu, taihojutsu (Japanese police immobilization and arresting methods), and Kodokan judo.

The founder of Nihon Jujutsu, Sato Shizuya, established this system based on his extensive studies with leading Japanese budoka (traditional martial artists), many of whom introduced ancient bujutsu methods to modern budo.

The list of the men with whom Sato Sensei trained directly or was influenced by reads like a compendium of the greatest Japanese martial artists of the 20th century:

Ueshiba Morihei (1883–1969). The founder of aikibujutsu and modern aikido.

Mifune Kyuzo (1883–1965). 10th-dan Kodokan judo, senior instructor at the Kodokan, and founding member of the International Martial Arts Federation.

Nagaoka Hidekazu (1876–1952). 10th-dan Kodokan judo.

Ito Kazuo (1889–1974). 8th-dan Kodokan judo, founding member and first Chief Director, Kokusai Budoin, International Martial Arts Federation (IMAF).

Kotani Sumiyaki (1903–1991). 10th-dan Kodokan judo, Director of the United States Air Force Strategic Air Command's combatives course at the Kodokan, and one of the Kodokan's foremost experts on judo kata.

Hosokawa Kusuo (1918–1997). 9th-dan judo, taihojutsu instructor of the Strategic Air Command's combatives course at the Kodokan.

Ishikawa Takahiko (1917–2008). Instructor of the Strategic Air Command's combatives course at the Kodokan, two-time All Japan Judo champion. Dedicated 30 years to establishing judo in North America.

Dr. Tomiki Kenji (1900–1979). Founder of the Japan Aikido Association and Shodokan-ryu aikido (also known as Tomiki-ryu aikido), 8th-dan Kodokan judo, 8th-dan aikido, chief aikido instructor of the Strategic Air Command's combatives course at the Kodokan.

After my having had to deal with senior instructors dodging or refusing to answer questions about their own or others' training histories, I believe it's critically important when purporting to offer training in authentic Japanese martial arts to be able to cite a readily-verifiable person-to-person lineage of instruction. Nihon Jujutsu can trace its roots to Daito-ryu Aikijujutsu, Tenjin Shinyo-ryu Jujutsu, and Kito-ryu Jujutsu.

Even more important to me is the fact that Sato Sensei selected the waza for his system from the techniques that had been taught to wartime military and civilian law enforcement for use in potentially lethal, hand-to-hand combat. While there is very definitely a strong focus on personal development and fitness in Nihon Jujutsu as the art exists today, the foundation on which the art is built is techniques that work when needed.

Suino Sensei teaching one of the many judo techniques included in Nihon Jujutsu.

As I wrote previously, our legacy practice of aikijutsu was heavily dependent on collaborative training, especially in the early years of training. Nihon Jujutsu most certainly does not rely on compliant training partners. Even in the early stages of learning a new technique of application, *uke* (the person "receiving" the technique) is encouraged to provide integrated structure and intentionality in their "attack," leading eventually to practice against serious, physical opposition. We're still adjusting to this paradigm, and it's not unusual to have Suino Sensei call out—even across a Zoom connection—"Stop just going-with the technique!" The huge upside for me is being able to share with my students techniques that work to start with, and that will only become more powerful and effective as students increase their levels of skill.

Kata practice in our legacy art of aikijutsu.

An integral aspect of Nihon Jujutsu that facilitates learning is the inherent logic and geometry of the techniques. From what I can see at this point, there are a limited and very manageable number of foundational principles that define movement patterns, and which pattern to apply is based on the position, in the moment, of uke. In other words, what uke does practically shouts at *tori* (the person applying the technique) which direction to go and what to do.

This is *very* different from our legacy art, in which techniques generally required a specific circumstance, out of all the myriad things that could be happening, and the "defender" had to identify almost instantaneously which technique to choose in response. Hence why the legacy aikijutsu was practiced purely as *kata* (choreographed forms) well into the black-belt ranks. Nihon Jujutsu students practice their techniques in semi-freestyle sparring almost immediately and are tested on that ability at the green-belt level. First-degree black-belt candidates must demonstrate spontaneous, freestyle sparring against multiple opponents "attacking" with any kind of strikes, grabs, or bear-hugs.

By contrast, first-degree black-belt candidates in the legacy aikijutsu are officially told to choreograph, supposedly secretly—which is to say, pre-plan and fake—the *randori* (sparring, in this case against a single uke) portion of their exam.

An aikijutsu technique. Spectacular, but highly cooperative.

Another especially appealing aspect of the Nihon Jujutsu logic and geometry is the ready availability of *henka-waza* (a variation, or change technique). A henka-waza is a means to continue a defense when the initial technique attempted is jammed, countered, or otherwise fails. Even in just Kihon Kata I, almost every technique has a reciprocal. If uke manages to stop tori's initial effort, tori can reverse direction and execute a technique appropriate to that momentary geometry. During another era in our storied past, in which we were the testbed for an eclectic approach to aikido, all waza were to be practiced in pairs, specifically to facilitate henka-waza. The problem was the techniques had been chosen, maybe not randomly, but without the inherent logic of the Nihon Jujutsu curriculum. Consequently, that approach did not develop the early facility offered by Nihon Jujutsu.

I'm also substantially enamored with the fact Nihon Jujutsu addresses all ranges of hand-to-hand combat: striking (punching and kicking), arm's-length grappling (aikibujutsu and jujutsu), close-range grappling (judo), and ground-fighting (newaza). While Itten Dojo students will not be as expert in any given range, compared to students at schools focusing entirely on only one of those ranges, they will be one heck of a lot more capable overall. The variety embodied in Nihon Jujutsu is not only hugely beneficial in its own right, the variety provides for much more engaging, long-term training.

Although we've not yet started in this portion of the curriculum, Nihon Jujutsu does include use of weapons. I had a chance to observe a bit of a class at JMAC, during which Gage Sensei was teaching techniques using the four-foot staff, just one of the weapons addressed in the art. The jo is one of my favorite weapons and, based on what I saw Gage Sensei doing, I can't wait to get into this aspect of the training.

Ultimately, the greatest appeal to me of Nihon Jujutsu is confidence in the art. As mentioned above, the foundational principles and techniques were chosen very specifically on the basis of demonstrated, practical utility in potentially life-threatening situations. Even with all my time in our legacy aikijutsu, I knew that if I ever had to defend myself, I would likely go straight to karate, the art in which I also had decades of training and experience with heavy-contact sparring. My perspective on that is also changing. I've only received a fraction of the Nihon Jujutsu curriculum at this point, but I can clearly perceive that the core techniques, the practicality of which is only enhanced by Suino Sensei's "real-time self-defense" applications, provide a go-to art, one that will serve the members of Itten Dojo eminently well.

I'm immensely grateful that the opportunity to train in Nihon Jujutsu has been opened to us.

16 REFLECTIONS

In the old Isshinryu Karate Club headed by Ralph Lindquist—where I earned my first black-belt and, more importantly, met my wife Rosanne, and subsequently Alan and Deb Starner—we had a saying: "If we ever saw anyone that knew more about this stuff than we do, we'd be training with them." That saying actually came to fruition, at least for some of us, and led the Wolfes and Starners to resign from the Isshinryu club and create Itten Dojo. After more than 30 years, the Wolfes and Starners are still together (both couples—plus daughters—and collectively!), Itten Dojo has become something more and very different than we ever imagined, and the future is unfolding with opportunities that beggar belief.

Before I go any farther, I want to acknowledge the many members of the dojo who are directly responsible for its continued existence—through not just the good times, but through multiple, black-swan events that would have been the end of any endeavor less enthusiastically supported.

Foremost is the late Bill Campbell. Mr. Campbell was the CEO of Campbell, Rodoff, and Stewart Food Brokerage and the primary owner of the building on Trindle Road in Camp Hill that originally housed Itten Dojo on the second floor of the offices.

I'm listing the following individuals in more-or-less chronological order of their initial black-belt promotions (many achieved black-belts in multiple arts), rather than by magnitude of individual contributions to the dojo (although all individual contributions have been significant, and in some cases have continued even though the individual now lives far away). These are the members that achieved black-belt rank: Alan Starner, Randy Manning, Ed Dix, Michael Rozycki, John Butz, Eric Fennel, Matthew Yohe, Dr. Michael Nickels, Carmen Altomonte, Peter Hobart, Don Dodson, Budd Yuhasz, Jevin Orcutt, Jennifer Bennett, Gary Burkett, Charles Hudson, and Dr. Sarah St. Angelo.

Unless you've done the same, in this dojo or elsewhere in an equally demanding environment, you have no idea the sacrifice and dedication these individuals invested to attain the ranks they achieved.

But there are others that, while not having achieved black-belt rank—or not specifically within our dojo—nonetheless made contributions without which the dojo would not now exist.

Josh Freeman heads the list. Josh had served in the Army Special Forces and eventually took over his father's very extensive real estate and development company. On several occasions, Josh provided critically-needed loans or direct financial support that carried us through. Just two weeks prior to his untimely death in a helicopter crash, Josh told me he had something in the works that would tie our two dojo closely together and permanently ensure the existence of both. I never learned what Josh was planning to do. The *Tomon*, the magnificent dojo he built, is long gone, but Itten Dojo embodies part of Josh's legacy.

Josh Freeman, at right, conversing with Ellis Amdur during the seminar weekend at Josh's Tomon dojo.

A number of former members, such as Scott Farrell, Jen Pomerantz, Liam McFarland, and Vic Wadhawan, have stayed in close touch and over many years have made donations of funds or unneeded gear, or provided expert professional services to the dojo, free of charge. Their continued support of the dojo is very deeply appreciated.

With just a few notable exceptions in the course of three decades—and no, I'm not going to cite them by name—everyone else that has held membership in Itten Dojo has had a positive impact and helped make the dojo what it is today. My electronic records extend back to 1996. Even missing the first four years during which I did not keep detailed records, it's clear that almost 2,000 people have inquired about training over the years, and more than 500 people have enrolled and actually trained—most of them for an extended period of time. The really important thing is that every member of the dojo has been known, deeply and by name, by the instructors and their fellow students.

And, there have been many senior instructors with whom the dojo has trained since 1992. Originally, we had no expectation of ever doing anything other than karate and kenjutsu. But Fate had other plans. Sometimes by intention, and other times in order to recover from one of those black-swan events, we've accumulated substantial experience and oftentimes rank in a range of arts, both *koryu* (old-style) and *gendai* (modern) budo. Most of the instructors with whom we've worked have been exceptional, as martial artists and as individuals but, as has been the case with members of the dojo, there have been a few notable exceptions. I learned a great deal from all of them—the positive examples have had characteristics I try to emulate; the others I take as examples of what to avoid being or doing under any circumstances.

I started to create a list of everyone with whom we've trained, and then changed my mind, deciding instead to just make a short list of the most positive, past influences on our dojo (some of whom have been mentioned already):

Ted Vollrath. My final karate instructor—he was the first person in the world to achieve black-belt rank from a wheelchair. And then he did the same in multiple arts. His non-profit "Martial Arts for the Handicapable" made training available to many individuals that otherwise would not have had the chance. Vollrath Sensei was a huge supporter of our dojo in its earliest years and a very significant mentor to me.

A JOURNEY OF SWORD AND SPIRIT

William Knight. My first kenjutsu and aikijutsu instructor, and a great friend. It was always the best fun when Knight Sensei started a mini-lecture with, "It's a paradox…"

Knight Sensei, in one of those "It's a paradox…" moments.

Diane Skoss. We spent many years commuting to New Jersey to train in koryu jodo, and enjoyed every moment working with Skoss Sensei. She's now a *menkyo-sha* in that art, and it is richly deserved.

Diane Skoss instructing Rosanne Wolfe and Deb Starner in Shinto Muso-ryu Jo.

Ellis Amdur. Collaborating with Amdur Sensei on an eclectic approach to aikido yielded an entirely different way to train and a wealth of insights. His writings continue to be very influential.

Rodney and Mitsuko Uhler. The Uhlers were responsible for enabling us to train in koryu kenjutsu and provided our introduction to and opportunities to train with the incomparable Okabayashi Shogen.

With Okabayashi Sensei and the Uhlers in Detroit, during Sensei's final visit to the U.S.

It's sometimes said, "The past is prelude," and that certainly applies to our dojo. We now have direct access to a number of the most highly qualified instructors in the world, and our dojo and arts are recognized and supported by international budo organizations based domestically and in Japan, including the Shudokan Martial Arts Association, the Reigakudo Foundation, the Yamabushi Jujutsu Aikijutsu Association, the Nihonden Aikibujutsu Senyokai, and the Japanese Budo Association.

Our in-house instructor staff has expanded to include:

Mark Hague guides our Ono-ha Itto-ryu Study Group—his martial arts career has spanned over 42 years, 19 of those years training in Japan. He started Ono-ha Itto-ryu at the Reigakudo under Sasamori Takemi in 2002, was awarded the *Kanajisho* license in 2009, and is the only licensed and certified instructor (*shidosha*) of the Reigakudo in the Americas.

Hague Sensei working with longtime dojo member Lonnie Dunham.

Rie Hashimoto Bailey, our instructor for *shodo* (calligraphy), as well as Japanese language and culture, has been a member of our dojo for more than a year already, and her teenaged children train in Nihon Jujutsu. Bailey Sensei's presence has added a unique aspect to our dojo that no other martial arts schools in this area can match. In addition to her wide-ranging expertise and great skill as an instructor, Bailey Sensei's bright spirit and energy illuminate our dojo.

In addition to teaching, Bailey Sensei regularly creates beautiful ikebana arrangements that grace the tokonoma in our visitors' area.

Our visiting instructor for iaido, jujutsu, and judo, and (as should be apparent to you by now) the person most responsible for the ongoing transformation and growth of our dojo is Nicklaus Suino. Suino Sensei has been called "one of North America's foremost martial arts teachers," and is highly-ranked in iaido, judo, and jujutsu (among other arts). His personal mission is to master the most profound aspects of Japanese heritage martial arts and offer the true Japanese budo experience to his students. Suino Sensei believes that proper practice of Japanese martial arts can have a profoundly positive effect on people's lives—and we can attest to this! Since 2009, he has been consulting for businesses and individuals who want to improve their effectiveness using the physical, mental, and intangible principles of mastery.

Suino Sensei is always accompanied on his visits to our dojo by several of his assistant instructors, a group of exceptionally talented martial artists that have given unselfishly toward our progress and have become great friends. These *sempai* (fellow students of Suino Sensei with whom we have a special relationship) include Daniel Holland, Jon Spengler, Nick Miller, Mike Mancini, Richard Monroe, and Amber Cathey.

Amber Cathey and Richard Monroe providing judo training hints.

Two other individuals have played hugely significant roles in establishing the reputation of our dojo. Most importantly, Mike DeMarco, the publisher of the *Journal of Asian Martial Arts*, not only accepted multiple articles written by me and other members of the dojo, but has been an advocate for our dojo over many years, and a very good friend. Another publisher, the late Angel Lemus, made me an assistant editor and frequent contributor to his *Bugeisha Traditional Martial Artist* magazine. Through their friendship and support, Mike and Angel have promoted our dojo to an international readership of serious practitioners of the martial arts.

Through the more than three decades of the existence of Itten Dojo and all that we've experienced and learned in that time, one lesson stands out most clearly. It's best summarized in another saying of the old Isshinryu Karate Club where this journey began: "It is the doing and the sharing of the doing that is the essence and true value."

We could not agree more.

APPENDIX—LAW OF THE FIST

Peter Hobart has very kindly contributed this immensely valuable addition to the book. Peter is a former bartender and a former state prosecutor who currently works for the United States government. He has been an avid student of the martial arts since childhood, when his father—a heavyweight Golden Gloves champion—first introduced him to "the sweet science." He is honored to be an itinerant member of the Itten Dojo, where he spent many happy years before moving south.

As a college student in the mid 1990s, I was compelled to buy a very expensive sword, and a very cheap car, in order to be able to make regular pilgrimages to Itten Dojo. On the day of my first visit, I hitched my metaphorical wagon to that star, and eventually found a job in Central Pennsylvania, moving my family there in order to continue to develop this special relationship. In the quarter-century-plus since that first fateful encounter, I have come to know this unique place—and its chief instructor—very well. Wolfe Sensei is a world-class martial artist and has an abundance of excellent qualities that are essential in a good martial arts teacher, but this section will focus primarily on three specifics (which are too often sadly lacking in this profession): combat practicality, legal knowledgeability, and personal humility.

The Crucible: In a realm where combat effectiveness is rarely tested, and even when tested, is often subject to restrictive regulations, it is hard to know what techniques truly will and will not work in reality (hence the old joke: Q. *"How many martial artists does it take to screw in a lightbulb?"* A. *"Three: One to do the job and a second to tell the third, 'That would never work in the street!'"*). Despite having expertise in some of the most esoteric and nuanced techniques in the entire martial armamentarium, Wolfe Sensei is adamant that students at Itten Dojo should actually learn how to protect themselves. For real. In an uncontrolled environment. And in every aspect of the battle. What aspects? Experts in violent encounters generally agree that there are at least three battlefields to be considered: The physical, the legal, and the psychological.

I. The Physical Battlefield: As you make your way along the martial path, there is good news, and there is bad news…

SAI WENG SHI MA

Once, a righteous man lived near the border. One day, for no reason, his horse ran off into barbarian territory, and everyone felt sorry for him.

But his father said: *"Who knows if that won't bring you good luck?"*

Several months later, the horse came back, bringing with it a group of noble horses, and everyone congratulated him.

But his father spoke: *"Who knows if that won't bring you bad luck?"*

His house now rich in horses, the man's son came to love riding, but one day, he fell from his mount and broke his leg. Everyone felt sorry for the man.

But his father said: *"Who knows if that won't bring you good luck?"*

One year later, barbarians invaded across the border. All the adult men strung up their bows and went into battle, in which nine out of ten were killed, but not the man's son, because of his broken leg…

Thus, bad luck brings good luck, and good luck brings bad luck. This happens without end and nobody can estimate it.

—Claude Larre et al., *Les grands Traités du Huainan-zi*, (Broché, 1993), p. 208–209

Some Bad News: There are many reasons to study the martial arts, only one of which is to learn practical, effective, realistic methods of self-defense. But if developing such an ability is among your priorities, there is a hard truth which must be accepted right out of the gate: You cannot think your way out of a fight (or as Mike Tyson so pithily puts it: *"Everyone has a plan until they get punched in the face."*). This is so, because when fists actually start flying, there is simply not enough time to formulate and execute a plan of action, and fighters inevitably revert to autonomic responses.

Some Good News: The body's instinctive reactions to a threat can be helpful or harmful depending on a multitude of factors, but for the most part, they can be modified with sufficient training and practice so that they tend toward the beneficial end of the spectrum. But the groundwork for surviving such situations—the careful re-shaping of instinctive reactions—must be laid long in advance of a violent encounter. And this takes time and training.

More Bad News: Unfortunately, just as proper practice prepares the participant to perform powerfully under pressure, improper practice can be worse than none at all. Conditioning students to rely on unrealistic or nearly impossible techniques when push comes to shove will cause them to try and fail, often leaving them in a worse defensive posture than if they had no training at all and simply fell back on instinct. Such poor training methods also contribute to an unwarranted sense of confidence, which can be just as dangerous as defective technique.

More Good News: Fortunately, the truth of combat is that the simplest techniques are almost always the best. In fact, perhaps the single most important thing that students of the martial arts learn in the dojo is not how to throw a punch, but *how to take one*. No matter how tough an individual may be, the first time he gets hit in the face, it will invariably cause a state of shock, often sufficient to prevent any further response. This is so not (necessarily) because of the power of the strike, but rather the novelty of the sensation (just ask any man over 50 who has had to undergo a full medical exam). Martial arts students, by contrast, are typically quite used to this feeling and know that they can keep on fighting after taking a hit.

A related concept is that martial artists are capable of *delivering* a strike. Before getting to the particular means and methods, however, it is important to explore the concept in general—having a mindset that allows you to inflict harm upon another when necessary and appropriate.

S.L.A.M.

Brigadier General Samuel Lyman Atwood Marshall, also known as S.L.A.M., was a military journalist and historian, who served with the American Expeditionary Forces in World War I before becoming a journalist, specializing in military affairs.

In his most famous publication, *Men Against Fire: The Problem of Battle Command*, he claimed that fewer than 25% of men in combat actually fired their weapons at the enemy. When asked why this was so, he explained that even when his own life is at risk, the average individual is reluctant to, *"kill...a fellow man...he will not...take life if it is possible to turn away from that responsibility and at the vital point, he becomes a conscientious objector."* Marshall's conclusions in this regard are consistent with the results of multiple studies performed by other military analysts between the 18th century and 20th centuries, although some of these analysts attribute the so-called "low fire rates" to a lack of training and discipline.

As simple as it may seem, overcoming these innate psychological barriers puts the practitioners of the martial arts streets ahead of the average person when it comes to combat. For next-level martial arts instructors, these initial steps also involve the delicate matter of forging the student's spirit.

The Perfect and the Good: Any complete, classical martial art employs a catalogue of techniques that will take a lifetime to master. What sets Itten Dojo apart from others, however, is that running parallel with the long-term effort to refine students' ability to perform this syllabus exquisitely, is the short-term goal of equipping them to survive in the street as quickly as possible. Like wilderness explorers in a hostile climate, students need to be able to develop some type of shelter from the elements immediately, and only then will they have the luxury of taking the time to build a more beautiful and enduring accommodation.

Tough Talk: One of the ways in which the wrong kind of martial training can do more harm than good is in the context of conversation. While you cannot think your way out of a fight, you can certainly talk your way into one. In some studios, tough talk and heavy contact contribute to the students developing a bit of an attitude, both on and off the mat. This is to be avoided for many reasons, not least because such heightened aggression is often paired with reduced ability—a truly deadly combination.

WALK ON

One of the toughest men I ever met—powerfully built, well-trained, combat-tested, and heavily scarred—once gave a brutal class on knife defense, at the conclusion of which, he asked, *"Do you know what I would do to a robber who pulled a knife on me and tried to take my wallet?"* The class was enthralled, anticipating all manner of devastating disarms and vicious counters, but this martial giant simply said, *"I would give it to him and walk away. There is nothing in my wallet worth risking my life or even another scar..."*

Most of my "non-dojo" experience with violence comes from three primary sources: I began my working life as a bartender; I then became a criminal prosecutor; and later in my career, I joined a special operations team. From these vantage points—in conjunction with many hours of world-class training on the mat at Itten Dojo—I have learned that there are, broadly speaking, two types of violence that you may encounter in the world that lies outside the dojo door:

Type I: First is the kind of sloppy, intoxicated, fisticuffs that often takes place in roadhouse parking lots at closing time. These encounters are generally preceded by a lot of posturing and insults, and characterized by a lot of grabbing and wrestling (known in the bar trade as "the walk around slowly dance"). They occasionally result in a black eye or a bloody nose—nothing a bag of frozen peas and a little sobering up can't cure. Throughout these ordeals, however, the combatants show what animal-handlers refer to as, "bite inhibition"—that is, an innate, humane level of restraint that allows for physical competition without the risk of total annihilation.

Type II: Second are brutal, sociopathic, rage-fueled criminal acts of unspeakable proportions, often resulting in torture and death. Clearly, those that inflict this kind of savagery on fellow humans exist well outside the norms of civilized society, and while such individuals are (thankfully) few, every serious student of the martial arts should learn to spot the difference immediately, and be prepared to respond accordingly. The close quarters combat training mantra of one particular agency that deals with offenders of this kind is: face-base-*coup-de-grace* (if you pronounce the French part with an American accent, you can make it rhyme).

But whichever type of violence you, as a martial artist, encounter, it is critical to be aware that after the physical battle has ended, the legal battle is just beginning. With this hard truth in mind, it is an essential aspect of the modern martial artist's training to develop at least a rudimentary understanding of the applicable laws if he ever hopes, or fears, that his training may be called upon outside the dojo.

The law can vary widely among jurisdictions even within the same country (let alone foreign nations), and it is constantly modifying and reinterpreting the applicable rules. As a result, it is important to be both specific and timely in your research and practice of this subject. The following selected categories, differentiating discrete aspects of criminal and civil law, are drawn primarily from jurisdictions located within the United States, and are intended only as a rough guide to the landscape. They do not—and cannot—constitute legal advice, and should not be relied upon as such.

II. The Legal Battlefield: Let's be very practical for a moment: What are the chances that a prudent martial artist will actually be called upon to use his or her self-defense skills in a real-world confrontation? Even if such a situation ever did arise, is it likely to happen more than once? Now compare this undeniably low probability with the chances that someone who is involved in a violent encounter will then be subjected to subsequent criminal or civil legal scrutiny (almost a certainty). Any instructor who has truly weighed these eventualities against one another will recognize that *much* more attention needs to be paid to understanding and applying the legal rules-of-engagement that govern the use of force in their particular jurisdictions. In this regard, as the inclusion of this material here and in on-the-mat training demonstrates, Itten Dojo leads the way.

<u>Criminal Law, Self-Defense, Non-Lethal Force</u>: Criminal liability is distinguished from civil liability in that it is the state which brings charges against the defendant, as opposed to the victim. The general criminal law in the United States allows for the use of necessary and proportionate, non-deadly force in self-defense anytime a victim reasonably believes that unlawful force is about to be used against him. The critical language under this standard is: **"reasonable belief," "unlawful," "about to,"** and **"necessary and proportionate."**

In order to establish a **reasonable belief**, courts will generally use both a subjective and an objective standard. The subjective standard determines whether this defendant truly believed that an attack was imminent (whether reasonably or unreasonably). In arriving at this conclusion, the defendant's state of mind is relevant. Thus, a paranoid defendant might introduce evidence of his condition to show that his belief, however unreasonable, was at least genuine.

But the reasonableness of the defendant's actions is judged by an objective, rather than a subjective, standard. The reasonable person standard is one of the most difficult aspects of the law to understand. In an effort to do justice to both sides, the law requires the trier-of-fact (usually the jury) to consider whether an ordinary person in the defendant's position would believe that force was about to be used against him. The defendant's (and the assailant's) physical characteristics and past history will be taken into account, but emotional fragility is of little or no concern. Thus, comparative size, weight, strength, handicap, or pre-existing injury may support a reasonableness finding, but unusual sensitivity or fear will not.

There is no simple formula for the legal application of force in self-defense in American law. The confusion is due, in part, to the complexity of the issue itself, and in part to the variety of state laws within the U.S. legal system. The requirement that the force defended against be **unlawful** simply excludes the right of self-defense when a so-called "assailant," such as a police officer, is legally authorized to use force. It must be noted however, that a majority of U.S. jurisdictions allow the use of force, including deadly force, in resisting an attack by a person not known to be a police officer, and the use of non-deadly force against a known police-officer attempting to make a wrongful arrest.

"About to" refers to the imminence requirement for the right to self-defense. It is not enough that the assailant threatens to use force in the future, or upon the happening of a certain event. Thus, the statement, *"If you do that one more time, I'll punch you,"* is likely insufficient to trigger the right to self-defense. The threatened use of force must be immediate.

The force used in self-defense must **reasonably appear to be necessary** to prevent the attack, and must be **proportionate** to the gravity of the attack. Thus, for example, if an assailant is about to slap the victim, responding with the use of a firearm would be excessive.

Criminal Law, Self-Defense, Lethal Force: The standard for use of deadly force is, predictably, much higher. The general criminal law allows for the use of deadly force anytime a **faultless** victim **reasonably believes** that **unlawful force which will cause death or grievous bodily harm** is **about to be used** on him.

The **faultlessness** requirement does not mean that the victim must be pure of heart and without sin. It does, however, mean that the right of self-defense will not be available to one who has substantially encouraged or provoked an attack. The general rule is that words alone are not enough to be considered a provocation under this standard, but there are exceptions. For example, saying, *"I am about to shoot you,"* might well constitute sufficient provocation.

One of the circumstances which helps to determine the level of threat encountered by the victim is the nature of the assailant's weapon (if any). As a general rule, anything which might be used to kill a person, no matter how odd, can be considered a deadly weapon. Thus, a chair, a lamp, or a screwdriver may all be considered deadly weapons. In some instances, the law will treat a trained fighter's hands as a deadly weapon, but in order to trigger the right to self-defense using lethal force against such a person, the victim must, of course, know of the attacker's special training.

U.S. courts are split with respect to an additional factor in the lawfulness of the use of deadly force in self-defense. A minority of jurisdictions require a victim to **retreat to the wall** if it is safe to do so, before using deadly force. "Retreat to the wall" is generally construed to mean taking any reasonable and apparent avenue of escape. However, even minority jurisdictions do not require retreat under three circumstances. There is no duty to retreat from one's own home; if one is being (or has been) robbed or raped; or if the victim is a police-officer making a lawful arrest.

Even an initial aggressor may be given the right to self-defense under certain circumstances. If the initial aggressor withdraws from the confrontation, and communicates this withdrawal to the other party, he regains the right to self-defense. Also, if the victim of relatively minor aggression suddenly escalates the confrontation to one involving deadly force, without providing adequate space for withdrawal, the initial aggressor may still invoke the right to self-defense.

Criminal Law, Defense of Third Parties: The right to defense of others turns largely on the reasonableness of the belief that the victim deserved assistance. A minority of U.S. jurisdictions require that the rescuer be a member of the victim's family, or the victim's superior or employee. Similarly, a minority of jurisdictions require that the rescuer's belief be correct, reasoning that the rescuer, "merely steps into the victim's shoes," while the majority requires only that such intervention is reasonable. If in the course of intentionally defending himself or another, a defendant recklessly or negligently injures or kills a third person, self-defense will not bar liability, but it may reduce the gravity of the charge from an intentional crime to a reckless or negligent crime.

Criminal Law, Defense of Property: In the majority of U.S. jurisdictions, a victim has the right to use non-deadly force in defense of his dwelling when, and to the extent that he reasonably believes that such conduct is necessary to prevent or terminate another's unlawful entry or attack upon his dwelling. Deadly force is authorized when violent entry is made or attempted and the victim reasonably believes that it is necessary to prevent an attack on a person within. It is also authorized when the victim reasonably believes that such force is necessary to prevent entry into the dwelling by one who intends to commit a felony therein. The rationale for allowing self-defense in these scenarios is based upon the right of inhabitants to be secure in their homes, rather than the right to defend property, as shown by the law regarding defense of uninhabited property.

Non-deadly force may be used merely to defend one's property from imminent, unlawful interference. Force may not be used, however, if some other, reasonable means would have the same effect. The only exception to the immediacy requirement is that force may be used to regain wrongfully taken property after the taking (i.e., no longer a prevention of immediate interference), provided that the victim uses such force in "immediate pursuit." The legal rationale for this exception is that the interference with the property continues for as long as the aggressor retains control of that property.

Deadly force may *never* be used purely in defense of uninhabited property. The popular misconception with respect to this law emanates from confusion over situations where the right to defend property and the right to defend the people therein overlap.

Criminal Law, Use of Force to Prevent Crime: As a general matter, a citizen has a privilege to use non-deadly force which reasonably appears necessary to prevent a felony, riot, or other serious breach of the peace, and some states (such as California) have extended this privilege to the prevention of any crime. Deadly force may be used only to prevent the commission of a dangerous felony involving a risk of human life. In some jurisdictions, a citizen has the same right as a police-officer to use non-deadly force to effectuate an arrest if he reasonably believes that the alleged criminal has in fact committed the crime. Similarly, in some jurisdictions, a private citizen may also use deadly force to effect an arrest in certain circumstances (provided the alleged criminal is actually guilty), but in this situation, a reasonable belief is not enough.

Civil Liability Generally: In a civil case, the victim (or his estate) brings the action. While there are many similarities to a criminal charge, it is important to understand that the civil plaintiff must only prove his case, "by a preponderance of the evidence." This is a much lighter burden than the criminal standard of, "beyond a reasonable doubt." The principal tort actions which a victim who defends himself might face, include assault, battery, and wrongful death.

Civil Liability, Assault and Battery: In virtually every U.S. jurisdiction, to make a case for battery, the plaintiff must show that the aggressor made harmful or offensive contact with the plaintiff's person; that the aggressor intended to bring about such contact; and that the aggressor's actions in fact caused the contact. While harmful contact is easily determined from the specifics of the situation, offensive contact is judged by the objective, "reasonable person standard." As a prominent Philadelphia law professor explains, "tapping a person on the shoulder is not reasonably 'offensive,' whereas tapping someone 'considerably lower down' could be." "The plaintiff's person" means anything connected to the plaintiff's body. This would include a hat, a cup in the plaintiff's hand, and on a bar exam question some years ago, even the car in which the plaintiff was sitting. Thus, snatching a book from a person might well constitute a battery.

The causation requirement can also be deceptive. Not only would a thrown projectile which strikes the plaintiff constitute a battery, but ducking to avoid such a projectile, and hitting one's head in the process, could also be civilly actionable. Moreover, no actual damage need occur to bring an action for battery. The mere offensiveness of a non-harmful contact can support an award of nominal damages.

Assault, briefly, is the creation of a reasonable apprehension of an imminent battery in the victim. Simple fear is not enough. The aggressor must have a present apparent ability to bring about such contact. In other words, the victim must actually expect to be struck or touched. Conversely, the fact that the victim was not in the least bit afraid does not bar recovery. Thus, a professional boxer may successfully sue a weakling for assault, even though there was no actual danger of being hurt.

Words are generally not enough to support an action for assault, but words coupled with some act may be. For example, shaking one's fist and threatening with words might well constitute assault. Similarly, a conditional threat such as, "Your money or your life," is also sufficient to support a charge of assault. Like battery, no actual damage need result.

Civil Liability, Wrongful Death/Survivor Actions: Although traditionally, any tort action abated at the death of the victim or the perpetrator, most states have now enacted "survival acts" for wrongful death claims (it is from this old common law rule that the bizarre concept of escaping liability by killing, rather than merely injuring a victim, is derived). Nowadays, however, the estate of the deceased can typically bring an action against the killer for all damages (e.g., pain and suffering) which occurred between the commission of the tort and death.

Further, every state has now enacted a statute providing for a civil remedy for wrongful death. Here, the designated representative sues the killer for the pecuniary injury to the next of kin (e.g., lost wages, lost companionship). While the wrongful death action is quite complicated, the critical aspect for present purposes is that the same defenses apply as if the victim himself were suing.

Civil Liability, Self-Defense in Tort Law: While the principles of self-defense in tort law are similar to those found in criminal law, the mode of analysis and areas of emphasis differ. In general, self-defense is valid when a person has reasonable grounds to believe that he is about to be attacked. Under these circumstances, he may only use such force as is reasonably necessary to protect against the potential injury. Since only reasonable grounds are required, a genuine mistake with respect to the attack will still support the right to self-defense. Once the attack has ended, however, so does the right to self-defense. Retaliation is never permitted.

As in criminal law, there is generally no duty to retreat, and deadly force may be used to prevent death or serious bodily harm. Even in the minority of U.S. jurisdictions which require retreat, there is an exception to the requirement if the victim is in his home. Although the attacker has no right to self-defense, if the attack is non-deadly, and the victim responds with deadly force, the aggressor may defend himself with deadly force.

Civil Liability, Third Parties: Under tort law principles, a victim who accidentally injures a third-party in the course of defending himself is also protected from suit by that third party. A majority of U.S. jurisdictions also allow a person to come to the defense of another only if the victim himself has a valid right of self-defense. Thus, if the rescuer makes a mistake regarding the victim's right to self-defense, he too will be liable. However, there is a strong modern trend toward protecting would-be rescuers from liability if their wrongful assistance of a victim is based on a reasonable mistake. When authorized to act at all, the rescuer may use as much force as the victim could have used in self-defense.

Civil Liability, Defense of Property: In the defense of property, a request to desist prior to the use of force is required, unless it would be futile or dangerous. There is almost never a right to self-defense when the "intruder" in fact has a right to be on the property. Thus, it is unwise to attack a supposed intruder without ascertaining his identity and purpose first. A significant exception occurs, however, when the "intruder" contributes to ambiguity regarding his identity or purpose.

As in criminal law, there is a right to use force in the recovery of stolen property, as long as the victim is in "hot pursuit" of the thief. Also as under the criminal standard, deadly force may never be used simply to defend property. Finally, the right to trespass for "necessity" supersedes the right to defend property under a self-defense theory. Thus, a home-owner is not privileged to use force to turn away those who trespass in order to seek refuge from an emergency.

Civil Liability, Prevention of Crime: Since the right to use force is limited to the prevention of the commission of a tort in civil actions, one who subdues an attacker, and then continues to use force to hold him until the police arrive, must be aware that he has moved over from a tort privilege to the privilege of arrest under criminal law.

Civil Liability, Agent of the Teacher: As a general matter, under the theory of agency, the "principal" or "master" is liable for unlawful acts which he causes to be done through an "agent," or "servant." There are three possible ways in which a martial arts instructor might be held liable as the principal for the unlawful acts of his students, as agents.

First, if the instructor appears to ratify or approve of unlawful conduct, he might be held liable for the commission of such acts. Thus, a dojo which encourages the use of excessive or lethal force in inappropriate situations may be seen to ratify and approve such unlawful conduct. Similarly, an instructor who continues to teach a student who has abused his knowledge may be held responsible, if not liable, for subsequent torts.

Second, an instructor may be held liable for having entrusted a student with, "an extremely dangerous instrumentality." "[W]hen an instrumentality passes from the control of a person, his responsibility for injuries inflicted by it ceases. However, when an injury is caused by an exceptionally dangerous instrumentality, or one which may be dangerous if improperly used, a former owner or possessor may...be charged with responsibility for [its] use..." 79 AM. JUR. 2D Weapons and Firearms § 38 (1975). The implications for instructors who teach potentially lethal techniques is clear.

Finally, an instructor may be liable for harm to the student or other parties as a result of negligent instruction. Anyone who holds himself out as an expert capable of giving instruction is expected to conform to the standards of his professional community. Thus, any instructor who, by his own negligence, fails to provide, teach, and require adequate safe-guards and supervision, may be liable for any resulting injury.

Conclusion: The law, and the facts underlying a cause of action, criminal or civil, are rarely clear-cut. Statutes and case law vary widely from jurisdiction to jurisdiction. Lawyers are skilled at recasting the facts in their clients' best interests. Juries are given broad discretion with respect to determining guilt or innocence, and may feel the need to compensate an injured party regardless of fault. And even if a defendant successfully raises one of the defenses discussed above, litigation is costly both in terms of time and money.

It would be foolish to try to rely on a general understanding of the legal principles at work in these situations in order to engage in behavior which falls just within the realm of legality. Rather, the wise martial artist will attempt to avoid any hint of liability or criminal conduct. The following general principles may be of value in this endeavor.

- Avoid physical confrontation. If there is a safe avenue of retreat, use it (regardless of jurisdiction). At a minimum, retreat to the wall if it is safe to do so.

- If confrontation is inevitable, give warning when defending property, unless doing so would be dangerous or futile. This does not mean that you should list your qualifications, as the samurai of old were wont to do. Rather, simply give the aggressor notice that you intend to use force against him in order to allow him to reconsider his position.

- Ensure that you are not seen as the aggressor. This does not necessarily require taking the first hit, but it does require being pretty confident that physical contact is imminent prior to reacting (for an in-depth examination of the danger here, see the Bernhard Goetz case).

- Be aware of the aggravating and mitigating factors. Is there a size, age, or ability differential? Are you or the attacker armed or trained? All of these factors will help you determine the appropriate level of force.

- Use only the amount of force necessary to deter the attack. This does not require the use of ineffective technique, but rather mature reflection prior to a confrontation about what technique (including flight) is appropriate in which situation. It would be wise to introduce this as part of regular training.

- Once the initial threat is neutralized, stop. This does not mean that you must give your opponent a fighting chance. Rather, you may immobilize your attacker while awaiting the police, but do no further damage.

- When intervening on behalf of a third party, ensure (as much as possible) that the intervention is justified and necessary. As a rule, interference in domestic disputes is unwise. Subsequent reconciliations can spell trouble for even the most well-intentioned, would-be rescuer.

- Remember that, in this country, human rights are superior to property rights. The use of force in the protection of property is very risky.

- As an instructor, you are both morally and legally responsible for the actions of your students, both inside and out of the dojo. Your regular training should encompass at least some attempt to address the legal rules-of-engagement and appropriate responses thereunder.

As a well-rounded instructor, you should know the law at least to the extent of whether your state is in the majority or the minority with respect to the issues raised above. If you do not have a lawyer or law student in your dojo, any law school library will have a copy of: *Your State Statutes Annotated* (i.e., *Texas Statutes Annotated*). Simply look in the index under the headings listed in this essay to find the applicable law.

III. The Psychological Battlefield: One of my current duties involves working with Special Agent trainees at Quantico. Year after year, I see that despite being the best-of-the-best, drawn from elite state law enforcement agencies and military elements, among their greatest fears is public speaking. I believe that one of the primary reasons for this deep-seated worry is concern about being wrong. Which is to say fallible. Which is to say human. Similarly, I believe that one of the greatest fears that martial artists harbor in relation to real confrontations (either inside or outside the ring), is not pain or injury, but losing. Which is to say weakness. Which is to say being human. Everyone is wrong sometimes. Everyone is weak sometimes. In the end, it comes down to protecting our fragile egos. Anyone who tells you that they know/are an invincible fighter is both arrogant and wrong, and in this regard, unchecked egos can be massively damaging to both training, and psychological equilibrium, before, during, and after a violent encounter. And here is where we return to the chief instructor of Itten Dojo. While skill, dedication, and ability are not vanishingly rare commodities in training halls across the nation, humility is (especially when the practitioner is skilled, dedicated, and able). In terms of this human characteristic that is so vital to developing the right mindset at all stages of training in, and deployment of, the martial arts, Wolfe Sensei has few equals.

I once had a Chief who would say in briefings, "Don't tell me what I already know or can guess; tell me what I don't know and haven't guessed." Here, then, is something you may not know (or have already guessed) about Wolfe Sensei and Itten Dojo:

In the decades that Wolfe Sensei has been training in the martial arts, he has earned very senior rank in several systems, gathered an astonishing breadth of knowledge and expertise, and developed a loyal student base that would follow him anywhere—this much you may already know. But, when faced with obstacles along the way, despite the obvious allure of simply declaring himself the head of his own system (as so many, less-well-qualified others have), Wolfe Sensei has consistently chosen the harder path, seeking out a series of world-class masters, despite being one himself. I believe that this is so because he exemplifies the best and most fundamental truth of the martial way: It is a journey, not a destination.

As you have learned in reading this excellent book, over the years and decades, through no fault of its own, Itten Dojo has encountered a number of turning points in terms of stylistic direction, and rather than simply resting on his formidable laurels and declaring artistic independence (which the vast majority of the school's members would have supported), Wolfe Sensei has always chosen a far more challenging way, voluntarily beginning the journey all over again at white belt, and working his way up through new systems with grace, skill, and humility.

The percentage of skilled practitioners who are willing to do likewise is small. The fraction of those who keep quiet about it is even smaller. And the number of those who have the courage to undertake such perilous journeys more than once—well, I know of only one…

If you too are seeking a lifelong journey rather than a terminal destination, you will find no better guide than one who has summitted the mountaintop from many faces, and no worthier text than one that whose title begins with the words: "A Journey."

DISCLAIMER: This analysis is not intended as a comprehensive statement of the law, or a legal opinion. It represents a general overview of the law, accurate to the best of my knowledge, at the time of publication. It should not be relied upon as a defense to any criminal or civil charges or complaints. In an effort to provide some practical guidance, this article addresses the current national majority position in the United States, and selected substantial minority positions regarding criminal and civil liability with respect to the use of force in defense of self, defense of others, and defense of property. The majority position reflects the practice of most states, and is increasingly consistent with the Model Penal Code (MPC). The author regrets the ubiquity of the terms "reasonable" and "generally" in this article—that these terms are essential merely reflects the complexity, and often the vagueness, of the law.

Peter Hobart during kenjutsu training, engaged in abdominal conditioning exercises at the original Itten Dojo.

ABOUT THE AUTHOR

Robert Wolfe, the founder and chief instructor of Itten Dojo, began martial arts training in 1975 and has taught since 1985. Wolfe has trained in swordsmanship since 1990 and aikijutsu/aikido/jujutsu since 1992. He holds the ranks of *rokudan* (sixth-degree black-belt) in aikijutsu, rokudan in Isshinryu karate, a kirigami *menjo* (certificate) in Ono-ha Itto-ryu (Sokaku-den) kenjutsu, was awarded a Bachelor of Arts Degree in Japanese Studies from Bucknell University in 1978; and is certified by the NRA to teach the Refuse To Be A Victim® crime prevention and personal safety seminars.

Wolfe retired from federal civil service after a long career supporting the U.S. Navy as a logistician. His final position was Director of Maritime Industrial Support, managing a staff of more than 40 individuals responsible for ensuring the proper material was delivered to the four Naval shipyards for on-time maintenance of nuclear submarines and aircraft carriers. A highlight of his career was receiving the Navy Meritorious Civilian Service Award, the third-highest decoration possible for civilian employees of the Navy.

As an author, Wolfe has published numerous articles addressing the martial arts in a variety of periodicals, ranging from popular magazines such as *Inside Karate, Martial Arts Training*, and *Aikido Today Magazine*, to internationally distributed, academic publications such as the *Journal of Asian Martial Arts*. He was an assistant editor and frequent contributor to *Bugeisha—Traditional Martial Artist* magazine.

Robert Wolfe and his wife Rosanne live in Mechanicsburg, Pennsylvania.